D1241861

The Devil at My Doorstep

*How I Survived a Three-Year War with
Big Labor and Protected My Employees
and Business*

David A. Bego

"Service Employees International Union President Andy Stern is the drama queen of Big Labor."

Wall Street Journal, July 16, 2008

"Our priority should not be to make unionized employers noncompetitive by raising the wages and benefits they offered their employees over the non-union company's wages in the market. Instead, our priority should be to *contribute* to our employers' success by organizing *all* their competitors."

A Country That Works

"We like conversation, but we embrace confrontation."

SEIU Executive Contracts Administrator Dennis Dingow to EMS President Dave Bego

Copyright ©2009, David Bego

ISBN-13: 978-0-9841457-0-6

Library of Congress Control Number: 2009931822

All Rights Reserved. No part of this book may be reproduced or transmitted in any form or by any means, electronic or mechanical, including photocopying, recording, or by any information storage and retrieval system. EMS employees' and others' names have been changed by the author to protect their privacy.

Beginnings

IT WAS A NASTY, UGLY, 3-YEAR, MILLION-DOLLAR WAR I DID NOT ASK FOR, but had to win. Otherwise, the business I loved would have been infiltrated by a scheming labor union determined to undermine employee privacy rights and destroy my version of the American Dream.

What is this Dream? Some may say it is a matter of freedom that allows every citizen in America the right to pursue a good life through free choice and hard work. Others use the term "equal opportunity" to describe the Dream—that all people should have the same chance to compete for any job without prejudice or threat. In this way, talent and skill become the tools of those who may succeed and discover peace and tranquility in their lives through a loving family, a comfortable wage, a nice place to live, and lasting friendships. Such a meaning coincides with the first use of the term by James Tousle in his 1931 book, *Epic of America*—"The American Dream is that dream of a land in which life should be better and richer and fuller for everyone, with opportunity for each according to ability or achievement."

Perhaps the Founding Fathers explained the American Dream best through the words, "life, liberty, and the pursuit of happiness." Such is only possible when no restrictions occur regarding any sort of class system, religious affiliation or the lack thereof, gender identity, sexual orientation, race, or ethnicity. Absent also must be the evils of greed, force, and power, for such things inhibit everyone's chance to live the Dream. This is why some sort of spiritual foundation is important because it permits a standard with which to evaluate conduct. This allows moral and ethical benchmarks to guide one's behavior, whether it involves personal choice or business decisions.

During a time of economic strife, many lose their belief that the American Dream is even possible based on several factors including loss of hope and lack of faith. Polls conducted by *Business Week* and *CNN* during the past two years or so indicated that from 50 to 66 percent of those polled believed the Dream was not achievable. Based on these perspectives, politicians during the 2008 Presidential election seized on the term, with the-then President-elect Barack Obama mentioning it often during the campaign, and at the Democratic Convention by comparing the phrase to basic "promises" with each person having the "freedom to make of our own lives what we will" while treating "each other with dignity and respect." Referencing businesses, he said, "[They] should live up to their responsibilities to create American jobs, look out for American workers, and play by the rules of the road." I couldn't agree more.

Whatever standard is used to define the American Dream, my station in life as the year 2006 rolled around certainly qualified me for having achieved this Dream as one who had played by "the rules of the road" in the true spirit of entrepreneurship. Starting with no customers, no office, and little capital to support the venture in 1989, I now own a commercial cleaning, facility maintenance and security business (nearly 5,000 employees in 33 states), Executive Management Services (EMS), based in Indianapolis, Indiana. Customers include nearly 50 Fortune 500 companies. Times were good as I enjoyed a loving wife and family including three children, a warm and comfortable home, good friends, and terrific relationships with both our company management team and the hourly-wage employees, 70 percent of whom were full-time. We provided workers with above-scale wages, vacation and holiday pay, and covered 80 percent of their health care costs while combating the hiring of illegal aliens with a strict background check system.

My spiritual compass was provided through my Catholic beliefs as a member of Holy Spirit at Geist Parish and a personal code of conduct—Christ-like in nature. I was involved in our local community as a volunteer and financial supporter for various charities including Indianapolis's critically acclaimed Children's Museum as well as the Special Olympics. EMS held an annual company golf tournament to raise funds for the YMCA's "Kids under Construction" project, St. Mary's Child Center, and Autism Advocates of Indiana. A second tournament called The Pete Dye Classic benefited the nationally acclaimed Riley Hospital for Children.

On the employee front, EMS hired mentally challenged people from Goodwill Industries and helped to fight muscular dystrophy resulting in our receiving the Golden Handcuff Award. Along the way, in 1995, Senator Richard Lugar recognized EMS as one of the fastest-growing companies in Indiana, and the City of Indianapolis honored EMS with the Eagle Award for its keen foresight and powerful wings that made it a success story. One year, I was a finalist for the Entrepreneur of the Year Award, an honor I sincerely appreciated because being an entrepreneur who started a company with nothing and helped it grow and sustain was indeed a special honor in itself.

Another benefit of owning our own business was the chance to incorporate family into the equation. One by one, those we loved had joined EMS in some capacity. These included my wife Barbara, brother-in-law Ray, sister Nancy, son Mark, daughter Kelly, son-in-law Matt, and even my father Robert. We were truly a "family business" in any sense of the term and this family extended to our management colleagues and front-line employees.

While we were proud of our achievements, EMS was certainly not going to change the world, but we were doing our part as a quality company with the motto, "We don't just clean, we manage." The big shot in our industry was ABM, and we were never going to topple them from power. In fact, we didn't want to do so. Instead, we concentrated on our focused businesses, cleaning services for buildings and plants, distribution of Barrett Supplies and Equipment (high-quality chemicals, equipment, and commodities) for 50-plus years a star in that industry, and security deployment through Delta Security Services. With offices in such states as Missouri, Georgia, Kansas, Indiana, Michigan, Pennsylvania, Florida, Ohio, New Mexico, Texas, and Arizona, we were proud of our customer service and spotless record as a provider of an important service to building and plant owners around the country.

Perhaps my proudest achievement aside from working with top management people who had been with the company an average of 15 years was the special relationship with EMS employees. Many of them did not have the chance to obtain university, college, junior college, technical, or even high school education, but they were good workers who believed in quality and hard work. How pleased I was that EMS could provide them with good-paying jobs and benefits fostering loyalty—since many of the employees had been with me for several years. It was never an "us" or "them" situation with me; it was "us" and "them," because we could not be successful without their help in providing the top customer service we rendered on a daily basis. EMS became known as a good place to work where employees received a square deal.

Since its creation, EMS had been union-free. In fact, the employees and I worked in an environment where freedom was the priority. I could run my company as I saw fit with input from both management and colleagues, and the employees could work in a free choice atmosphere without any threats to their security or safety. Even after nearly 20 years of being in business, I had not even considered the possibility that our employees were interested in a third-party representative (a union), as I had never been approached about any such development. If there had been interest, I would have gladly worked with the employees under the time-tested and preserved right to vote in secret with no threat of repercussion based on an employee choice. This is how general elections are held. Why should a union election be any different? Soon an interloper (the SEIU) would appear that believed the basic American right to vote privately was unfair—to the SEIU's financial well being!

Together, employees and management co-existed in our little corner of the world with wages a dollar an hour more than the union was providing its members and benefits fair to everyone. We did our best to do a good job for our customers and used the money we earned to pay our bills, educate our children, provide for our families, and help those who were experiencing difficult times. A simple situation really, with management and employees happy and carefree, living at least what many would call the American Dream.

If you can imagine this scenario, then try to imagine what it was like when one day this peaceful world was interrupted by the knowledge that EMS was about to be invaded by an outside adversary threatening to turn this world of ours upside down. One minute, we were enjoying the fruits of our labors minding our own business, and the next, attacks began lambasting the company as a "rat contractor" that cleaned buildings dubbed "Houses of Horror" for janitors who were exploited, intimidated, threatened, and abused all in the name of corporate greed. For the first time in our history, multiple National Labor Relations Board filings, frivolous charges with questionable evidence, would be filed against us for alleged employee rights violations and for supposedly firing union supporters as the EMS image was dragged through the mud.

As for me, I would be called deceitful, greedy, anti-union, and downright evil as noisy demonstrations and protests began popping up at buildings across the country where we managed the cleaning process. Letters packed with insults were sent to customers telling them what a scoundrel I was, one who profited from paying poverty wages. Based on these characterizations, imagine if you will, how you would feel when a sledgehammer begins to pound at your very being and you realize a large headache is about to infiltrate your brain for a long time to come. If you can imagine this situation, then you can relate as to how it felt when a super-charged, powerful, politically-connected, well-funded labor union, specifically the Service Employees International Union (the SEIU), decided to target us and wage war with a company that for almost 20 years had treated its employees with respect and dignity and those employees, with few exceptions, to a person, wanted no part of union organization within the company. Clergy groups, activist organizations, and even the Islamic community would enter the fray in support of our enemy, armed as they were with less than the truth but a belief we were the bad guys. News of the war would spread to London and beyond as the battle escalated by the day.

But wait, during a war dubbed by the union as a "Corporate Campaign" against EMS that would last three years and more, there was a ready aspirin-like remedy possible to cure this headache of mine. All I had to do was cave in to the union's demand that I sign a "Neutrality Agreement" indicating my agreement to "establish a recognition procedure for all of the company's non-supervisory janitorial employees." Even though this sounds innocent enough, it would have eliminated my employees' ability to vote through the historically important American right to the secret-ballot election. Instead, the procedure dubbed "card check" would have been used to determine if a majority of the employees (50 percent + 1) wanted union representation. In essence, the Neutrality Agreement was simply a precursor for something called the Employee Free Choice Act (EFCA), the legislation currently under consideration by Congress.

If I signed the document placed in front of me, I would instantly be transformed in the union's eyes from an ogre and threat to the union movement to the best friend of the union President, Stern. In effect, the union would view me as one who truly cared about and loved his employees, characteristics that were already true despite allegations to the contrary. No longer would I risk losing customers and ultimately be forced to lay off management and valued employees, or even potentially face bankruptcy because of lost revenues. Sign the paper and cave in to union demands as many other businesses had done during the SEIU's assault on our industry, and my troubles would be over. I would become a member of the "responsible contractor" family, the union's euphemism for a union contractor.

Yes, just a signature on a piece of paper, just one stroke of the pen, and my American Dream could continue without interruption. No more threats, intimidation, sullying of my reputation or the company's, no more filing of unwarranted complaints with government agencies such as the NLRB or OSHA (Occupational Health and Safety Administration), and no more angry words with union leaders as the SEIU could attempt to organize my employees using the card check method. All I had to do was say, "yes," but I couldn't simply sign that paper because doing so would have been against everything I believe in as an American citizen in a democratic country governed by the Constitution and the Bill of Rights. If I signed, I knew I would lose every bit of respect for myself, and the respect of those who knew what kind of a true patriot I was. With this in mind, I said "no," and shortly thereafter the war began in earnest, an ugly, costly, nasty, demeaning, no-holds-barred war threatening to ruin the company I loved. Yes, at risk was my American Dream; everything I had worked for from the day I started with nothing more than a willingness to work hard. Threatened with destruction of that business, I decided to fight back against the devil at my doorstep.

Labor History

Anyone who calls me anti-union simply doesn't know what he or she is talking about. Labor unions are an important part of American industry, and when their leaders truly are interested in the welfare of workers, the positives may outweigh the negatives. A step back into the past reveals many strong arguments in favor of union existence, and I am one who has always believed in learning from the past.

Rev. Martin Luther King believed the union movement had earned high marks.

• • • • • • • • • •

History is a great teacher. Now everyone knows that the labor movement did not diminish the strength of the nation but enlarged it. By raising the standard of millions, labor miraculously created a market for industry and lifted the whole nation to undreamed of levels of production. Those who attack labor forget these simple truths, but history remembers them.

• • • • • • • • • • • • •

Two Presidents—one from each political spectrum—agreed with Dr. King's view. John F. Kennedy wrote, "The American Labor Movement has consistently demonstrated its devotion to the public interest. It is, and has been, good for all America." Dwight D. Eisenhower believed "only a fool would try to deprive working men and women of their right to join the union of their choice."

And finally, words from the man I was about to wage war with, SEIU President Stern, "Today I send this message to every emerging global corporation: justice, family, community, and union are the same in every language and, wherever you go and whatever you do, a new global labor movement is coming to find you."

As I soon learned Stern meant what he said, that he and his union organizers were coming after me and my unsuspecting employees, and although most folks might be more familiar with the AFL–CIO, or the Teamsters Union made famous by their infamous leader James Riddle Hoffa, the Service Employees International Union had at least four important elements necessary to launch its crusade to infiltrate every global company: strength, power, money, and perhaps most importantly as I took them on, political power. Was I truly the "fool" President Eisenhower described above? Was I being foolish in trying to dodge the SEIU, to keep them off our property and out of our business, to deny them what they believed was their right to unionize EMS? When organizers first contacted me in 2006, these were questions I asked with no clear answers readily available.

To better understand why I made the choice I did, one must understand how unions evolved in this country and what they were established to represent. Once this is clear, then focusing on the SEIU, their evolution, and their march toward power and political influence follows.

To be certain, labor unions were the product of the endless relationship between workers and management stretching back to the early seventeenth century when English planters founding Jamestown complained about the lack of laborers available for duty. In 1786, just a year before the Constitution was adopted, Philadelphia printers staged a strike over lack of a good wage. A few years later, carpenters from the City of Brotherly Love did likewise based on their desire for a 10-hour work day "bill of rights."

Unions were first formed about this time, but they didn't band together in force until after the Civil War with the formation of the National Labor Union and the Knights of Labor. In 1886, London-born Samuel Gompers organized the American Federation of Labor (AFL) and fought to secure shorter hours and better pay for members through organization and collective bargaining. By 1904, more than a million seven hundred thousand members belonged, including those with various occupations including building laborers, musicians, electrical workers, and other skilled crafts.

More than 40 years later, John L. Lewis would add to the union movement with the establishment of the Committee for Industrial Organization (CIO). Lewis backed F.D.R. for President to the extent of telling workers "The President wants you to join the union."

After World War II, the two labor unions merged as the AFL–CIO with Lewis at the helm. Prominent during this time was also the United Auto Workers led by Walter Reuther. He organized major strikes in 1946 while rooting out any Communist infiltration.

Restrictions on union activities occurred a year later through adoption of the Taft-Hartley Act. President Harry S. Truman called it a "slave labor bill," and vetoed it before it became law. The bill addressed concerns over unfair labor practices, jurisdictional strikes, and picketing. In 1955, powerful leader George Meany was chosen to lead the AFL–CIO. Based on his resolve, four years later the Labor Management Reporting and Disclosure Act was passed establishing a bill of rights for unions because of concerns over the ingestion of organized crime figures into the mix. Free speech and assembly were guaranteed along with safeguards from unworthy punishment, the right to vote regarding dues, and the right to participate in union activities. More democratic rights thus existed in addition to standards being established to protect union funds. Guidelines to elect leaders were secured through fair and non-arbitrary elections. Transparency was the call of the day with members having the right of notification 15 days before elections. No union funds could be used for promotion of candidates with elections held at least once every three years. Most importantly, to hinder any repercussions against members concerning their voting rights, voting was required to be completed by secret ballot with impartial election observers alongside to make certain no corruption occurred.

Such safeguards were essential to union members' rights because the goal was for the union to protect interests regarding working hours, wages, and especially work conditions. Soon nearly every occupation had representation including police officers, airline pilots, doctors, writers, film producers and directors, actors, teachers, and factory workers. Instead of individual members having to secure their rights, the union was established to do it for them through collective bargaining and other procedures. People did not feel they were alone, but had the strength of unity behind them especially when grievance situations occurred. Then the union stood up for the little guy or gal and represented their best interest. What could be more American that this?

Companies that chose to recognize union representation could do so, or a majority of the workers could decide to unionize. Any attempt by the employer to dissuade union formation through threats or intimidation, or especially recrimination such as firing employees who advocated unions, was strictly forbidden. The flip side was that unions could not threaten or intimidate workers into forming a union, one specific reason for the evolution of the secret-ballot vote, a true protection providing the guarantee of freedom of choice for each worker. When union members felt they were being unfairly treated, the right to strike permitted them power and leverage to gain the changes they felt necessary at the particular business.

Under the National Labor Relations Act of 1935, Congress had permitted workers the freedom of choice to be represented if they wished to do so, provided them protections against discrimination, and created a board to oversee management–union disagreements regarding their legality. Despite these protections, unions fell into corruption during the reign of certain labor leaders such as James Hoffa, who many felt were more interested in lining their own pockets with gold than caring about the union members. Crusaders such as Attorney General Robert Kennedy sought to rid the unions of such leaders, and during the early 1960s, Hoffa and others landed in prison for their crimes. Violence and intimidation had been Hoffa's calling card, but his imprisonment did not stop more violence occurring in 1970 when United Mine Workers reform candidate Joseph Yablonski was murdered at his Pennsylvania home. This decade also witnessed the United State Postal Service mass strike and the United Farm Workers protests, led by César Chávez, against California Grape Growers. In 1979, the ruthlessness of employers bent on destroying unionizations was characterized in the successful film, *Norma Rae*, starring Sally Field.

In the late 1970s, more than 20 million workers belonged to unions marking an all-time high. During the 1980s, the plight of workers was once again front and center when Lech Walesa, later to win the Nobel Peace Prize, led a group of Solidarity workers protesting government intervention at the Gdańsk Shipyard in Poland. Nearly a year later, the air traffic controllers struck over rejection of a government contract with the-then President Ronald Reagan dismissing them at will.

As the 1990s progressed into the early part of the twenty-first century, unions, based on a number of factors, declined in importance with union membership in the range of 16 to 17 percent, or lower. Strong shifts in job location also began to affect the work force as more jobs became available in the western and southern states where union organizing was more difficult. Women's entry into the work force in larger numbers was also a contributing factor as fewer women normally joined than men.

Many of those noting the decline of union influence in the United States laid the blame squarely on management, but other factors had an impact on the decline as well. Certainly, the increase of foreign competition as well as the deregulation of many industries including airline travel, trucking, and rail shipping led to uncertain times. Foreign imports, the enemies of many companies who have seen their profits decrease due to the global ability to underprice American goods and services, also contributed to the crisis. Management, in turn, complained that if the union demanded high wages, excessive health care benefits, and unwarranted retirement security, cost of goods increased substantially and the company could no longer be competitive. In 2008/2009, this was the cry from those lamenting the demise of the American auto industry where many workers, including those paid with an hourly wage and benefits, were earning more than 65 dollars per hour.

All of these factors and more led to decreases in union membership and thus decreased revenue from dues. During the mid-twentieth century, more than 30 percent of the work force belonged to unions compared with less than 15 percent in 2004 and about 12 percent now, with many of those being government or public workers. One thing to remember—unions like SEIU are businesses too, non-profits yes, but businesses that must worry about the bottom line like any company existing today. They depend on revenues just like a normal business does to continue to exist. The revenues from dues are the lifeblood of the union along with donations or support from other entities. But unlike normal businesses operated with a capitalistic approach fighting for market share, the unions, at least the SEIU, operates under a structure replete with questionable tactics while using threat and intimidation as their calling card so as to impose unionization on those companies like ours who don't want, and really don't need, them around. It's like forced marriage, telling someone they have to link up with another person they don't want in their life. And, in SEIU's case, doing it with underhanded business practices, deceptive statements, and other means that are just a smidgeon short of being illegal because officials always allege wrongdoing, but avoid objectively false accusations. Employees targeted are often naïve, easily manipulated, easily intimidated, have an ax to grind, or have a chip on their shoulder and are willing to give up their freedom and let themselves be controlled by union organizers who are much more interested in their own survival.

In effect, many of the unions like SEIU have been trying to sell a product the American people don't want or need to buy. When EMS had an accountant take a gander at how the SEIU spends its money, he remarked, "What a sleazy group," as very little of the hard-earned money goes directly to helping the plight of the union members in the form of wage increases, benefits, and other matters improving working conditions. Many times unions like the SEIU take advantage of people who are misinformed and unfortunately believe much of the propaganda Stern and his colleagues pitch at them, especially those at entry-level positions like janitors, food service workers, security guards, day-care center helpers, etc. If they took a close look at why they joined the union in the first place, and whether their way of life has really improved, they might reconsider being a union member especially at companies like EMS where the employees enjoy their jobs because they are treated right from the day they are hired.

In the non-manufacturing sector where businesses such as EMS operate, union leaders nevertheless decided to take decisive action to fight back and restore unions to their rightful place. One such leader was Stern, who as the newly elected President of the SEIU, separated it from the AFL–CIO in 2005 when they would not back his reforms. The table was thus set for the controversial Stern and his union to begin a crusade to unionize as many non-manufacturing companies as possible. As a part of this strategy, EMS was squarely within the SEIU's crosshairs.

Foundations for Success

Wₕₑₙ Executive Management Services was created in 1989, I was a far cry from the young fellow who had earned a basketball scholarship to attend Wabash College 18 years earlier. Instead of concentrating on throwing a round ball through a hoop, I was about to risk everything my wife and I owned to become an entrepreneur in every sense of the word. Though the risk was apparent, we were ready to step to the forefront and try to be independent by owning our own business. Yes, I was ready, and my wife knew I was ready as she lent her support from every direction.

The aspiring executive whom she supported was born in Beech Grove, just south of Indianapolis, in September 1953. My mom, Phyllis, a Catholic who attended Sacred Heart High School, and dad, Robert, were both natives of the large city. They had married in April 1951, the same year the Korean War escalated to the extent that North Korean troops drove across the 38ᵗʰ Parallel and captured Seoul, and General Douglas McArthur was relieved of his Far East command.

Early days were spent around Lawrence, an Indianapolis suburb, while dad worked for a finance company. When

I was 10, he was transferred north to Fort Wayne, Indiana and we left the home of my birth. But I would never forget the days when dad was not only the coach of our baseball team, but drove the team bus as well. I played well enough to make the all-star squad and our teams often won the league championships.

Dad was a good man and compassionate, but he also really pushed kids hard. Mom was a great sport enthusiast too, and she never missed a game. When I was playing, I could always make out her voice, as she was one of the loudest cheerleaders in the stands.

All kids should have great parents like I did. Together, they showed me how to be driven and persistent in different ways. Mom, a real tomboy who wouldn't back down from anyone, was the more outspoken of the two. She was such a vibrant and outgoing person, one who had been a natural athlete playing sandlot baseball and football with the boys in the neighborhood. Later, she played girls basketball, but it was a far different brand of the game than the one competed at today on the high school or collegiate level. When mom played, all the team members couldn't even cross the 10-second line at the same time.

Dad was not a very tall man (5-foot 9-inches), but he liked basketball even though he didn't play regularly until he was a high school sophomore. He loved baseball and was a voracious reader, with history and sports his favorites. But dad wanted me to try all the sports, and when I was just an 8-year-old freckle-faced kid, he took me to Heather Hills Golf course (later named Maple Creek Country Club), the first one built by the gifted golf course architects Pete and Alice Dye. During the summers, I balanced playing golf, baseball, tennis, and even some football while being a part of teams through fifth grade. Looking back, I am sure sports instilled in me a sense of competition, of winning and losing, of being a good sport, of playing by the rules, and of never giving up even when I did not do well. I thank Mom and Dad for that experience because it helped mold the man I was to become when I entered the business world years later. But sports weren't my only passion—I used to love to drift over toward the area where Fort Harrison was located, wade the creek on the Army grounds, and play in the woods until the Military Police chased me off. What fun that was.

Before the family moved to Fort Wayne, a defining moment occurred when mom convinced dad to turn Catholic. From that day forward, Catholic schools like St. Lawrence in Indianapolis and St. Henry in Ft. Wayne were my home. Sports were the call of the day once again with dad as the coach of the baseball team and mom cheering us on. My sister Nancy was also a sports lover.

As 1967/1968 appeared, years when Middle East tensions and Dr. Martin Luther King's assassination caught the world's attention, my days were spent at Bishop Luers High School. Sports were once again my passion, but I recall trips to Washington D.C. or the mountains of Colorado where we took in the historical sites and relished togetherness as a family. But one strong recollection from these formative years occurred on the basketball court. When, as just a sophomore, I made varsity and played a great deal, some of the older players resented the attention coming my way. When one of them knocked out my front tooth one day with a vicious elbow, I woke up to the realization that not only did one competing have to play hard, but one had to be ready to face adversity by developing an inner-toughness and mental toughness to withstand the rigors and punishment involved. And alongside this type of toughness, a certain physical toughness was required so I could withstand the beating a player takes, especially those who are tall and play toward the basket. Slowly lessons of life were permeating my existence, ones that would be helpful later when the business world threw curves at me I never thought possible. Ones, yes, like those Stern and SEIU brought my way.

One evening during my senior year, when I had blossomed to nearly 6-foot 3-inches tall, dad told me a story regarding the progress made on the basketball court. He said he was sitting next to a fellow in the stands. When I made a good play, the guy said, "You know, that kid's got a lot of ability. I wouldn't be surprised if he isn't All-City and the city-scoring champ and goes on to play in College." And, as it turned out, the fellow was right. All this occurred and presto, I was offered a full-ride scholarship to play ball at Wabash College, just northwest of Indianapolis. Being able to persevere by being mentally tough had paid off and I could tell my parents were as proud as any parents could be.

I better backtrack a bit or I will get in trouble with a certain girl named Barb that I met during my junior year in high school. She had helped organize a hay ride, and although I was dating another gal, I noticed Barb right away. Who wouldn't have with her charm, enthusiasm, and natural beauty?

After some hesitance, the courage to ask Barb out on a date came to me. We were a year apart; I was 17. Thus began the romance of my life as we continued to date through high school before I left for Wabash. Despite my having little idea of what the future might be like, I popped the question two years later. To my delight, Barb said "yes," and we have been together ever since.

I was away at Wabash beginning in the fall of 1971, when the Vietnam War was raging, Richard Nixon was elected President and the general public became fascinated with the Watergate break-in. The experience taught me to be on my own. I joined the fraternity Beta Theta Pi and learned what it was like to live among guys who had different backgrounds and ideals. Listening to them talk about their dreams was illuminating; every fellow had a different path he wanted to follow. Mine was directed toward being a teacher with my major, of all things, German, an area of interest I had picked up from Dr. Planitz, head of the Wabash German Department.

Coaching was a main interest and I paid close attention to how our coach worked with the players as he attempted to mold us into a team. Perhaps without realizing it at the time, I picked up tips as to how to manage people by treating them fairly and listening closely to their ideas and suggestions.

Wabash was a grand experience, but during my sophomore year, the coach left and I decided to transfer to Tri-State University, north of Fort Wayne. They offered a good scholarship, although transferring meant sitting out a year under NCAA regulations. No matter, Barb and I were pleased as we were closer to both of our parents. No German major was available, but a professor told me he thought my capabilities might be with science, even to the point of becoming a doctor. Wow, Dr. David Bego—I liked the sound of that!

Moving on after graduating with a degree in biology, Ball State was next on the education front. Armed with enthusiasm toward the medical field while earning a Master's degree, I studied for the medical boards and did well enough to be interviewed for further study at Indiana University's superb medical school. But the dream of becoming a doctor was stifled with notification that I was listed as an alternate.

Disappointment reigned for a few days, but bouncing back had always been my way, and without hesitation, I decided to join the Central Soya Company as a research specialist in their experimental feed mill. When I joined the business world, how fortunate I was to have parents, both mine and on Barb's side, to emulate when it came to working with others and understanding how integrity and self-worth were the building blocks to success and peace of mind. My dad might have been a sports enthusiast, but he was a hardworking, smart businessman, and one who understood finance. Together, he and mom taught me the need to do things the right way, to carry myself with honesty, character, and integrity. My Catholic education also reinforced these values as an individual—a solid spiritual foundation is the cornerstone of anyone who wants to grow and learn. Barb's mom and dad, also Catholic, were good-natured, simple people from the farmland east of Fort Wayne. Her dad worked in a valve factory and was a postman while her mom stayed home and took care of the family. They, like my parents, brought love and caring ways into our souls, and taught us to put our faith in the Good Lord and trust the wisdom so important to daily life.

All this life experience was carried into the first job at Central Soya where I was appointed a supervisor in the experimental feed mill. The pay was decent as the employees and I tested different feed additives and new processes and machines to produce feed faster, more economically, and with better quality and better results. We worked with nutritionists and scientists who formulated feeds from a nutritional standpoint providing more durable feeds resulting in less waste and better conversion for the farmers. We set up experiments, monitored them, and prepared reports. Under my supervision were 10 union people, grain millers, who worked at a plant nearby. At some point, there was a strike and I watched carefully how the process worked—all with respect, as my grandfather had been a truck driver and a member of the Teamsters, and my uncle, a printer and member of his union for a while. Whether an employee was union or not made no difference to me—they would get a square deal based on their willingness to work hard and follow the plant rules.

One important lesson I learned occurred when a union member named Gary who was a tough cuss caught me not wearing my hard hat during a walk across the plant to talk to my boss. With a look of disfavor on his roly-poly face, he took his hard hat off and slammed it on the ground while saying, "If you don't have to wear your hard hat, I don't either." Realizing this was a strong challenge to my authority by a man who was probably 15 years or so older, I walked over and slowly but deliberately picked up his hard hat. Looking Gary straight in the eye, I boldly told him, "Don't you ever do that again. If you do, I'm going to write you up and I'm going to take you down the discipline path. C'mon, let's not start off like this. I'd rather work together with you than against you."

Gary stood silent for a couple of beats while I nervously waited for his reply. Perhaps my height and girth helped me a bit, but without hesitation, Gary put the hard hat on, smiled at me, and walked away. From that day on I never had another problem with any of the guys working for me.

Apparently my management skills must have impressed the powers that be, because within about 18 months, I was offered a plant superintendent's job in Michigan. The plant was unionized, and once again, I was able to learn how unions worked. I appreciated what they were trying to do for the employees and worked with them when problems occurred. Each day, I had experiences teaching me more about management and how to work with employees to improve production. My philosophy was simple—if they did well, the company did well, and then we all did well as profits were good, causing management and the big bosses to do well. Smiles all around.

Right away, I realized that the Michigan plant-working conditions were a mess—dirty and unfair to the workers. Several factors contributed to this, and I made it my priority to clean up the plant. One worker named Gerald, a rebel of sorts, wasn't exactly a fan of mine. His dad was a big-shot farmer in the area, but they didn't get along so Gerald worked for us. One day, he walked into my office with a sour look on his face and told me he "wasn't paying attention" and had made a huge mistake mixing dairy feed with hog feed. He told me with emphasis that I needed to call the home office and get some advice as to what to do. I cleared my throat, thought a minute, and then replied that I didn't need to call, but instead "Here is what we're going to do. I want you to get a ladder, safety harness, rope and some buckets, and I want you to go get your best friend in the plant, lower yourself into the bin, shovel off the feed that's on top into buckets, have your friend hoist it up and put it in the bin next to it." Gerald's eyes bulged a bit and he looked at me like I was crazy, but before he could answer I told him that the mistake was his responsibility and next time he should be more careful. He kind of snarled at me before leaving. About half an hour later, I went to check on what was occurring, and sure enough, there was the guy I knew as Gerald's best friend working with him separating the feed. The process took a couple of days, but Gerald learned a good lesson, that he had to take responsibility for his own mistakes. And I learned that instead of getting upset with employees who make mistakes, the better way was to simply work with them to correct the problem with mutual respect as the cornerstone.

A move cross-country was next in line for Barb and me. The decades of the 1980s, when Presidents Jimmy Carter and Ronald Reagan ruled the political world, had just begun when Central Soya transferred me to their Abilene, Kansas plant. But a true blessing had occurred as well with our daughter Kelly joining the family. She and Barb stayed in Michigan for a time as I approached the new plant with caution as no worthy management/employee relationships were in place. To make it even more difficult, the previous plant manager had apparently abused some of the employees. The camaraderie was nil, and worse, the plant was filthy with break rooms and locker rooms unsightly. Needless to say quality, production, and customer service were low!

From day one, I first began to learn about the employees and attempted to secure good solid, but arms-length relationships with them. Paramount was making them feel as if they were members of a team as we cleaned up the break rooms, locker rooms, warehouse, the production floors, and patched leaks in the roof where raindrops fell through. Slowly, the employees responded to the fair treatment and quality improved. We addressed a problem with inadequate lighting, but my boss wouldn't budge when I asked for help. To raise the money necessary, I sold a big pile of scrap equipment to a local junk dealer to purchase and install high-pressure sodium lights in the warehouse so the employees could see and do their jobs safely and productively, which held with my belief that if you treat people right, they will treat you right. My boss was happy also, because I killed two birds with one stone, improving work conditions and getting rid of an obscene pile of junk.

Within a year, we had turned the plant around and instead of it being in the bottom five, production-wise, it was now in the top five. There were no grievances filed and employee problems were few. When the employees screwed up, I called them on it, but they knew I was going to be fair and not kick them when they were down. One such example was with a warehouse fellow nicknamed Tex. I was walking through the warehouse one afternoon after lunch and I caught Tex, a mid-fifties guy sitting on a bag of feed sleeping. I gently nudged Tex's foot with my toe and he came awake wide-eyed and screamed, "Please don't fire me." I said, "Tex you know me better than that, but I need you to set an example for the rest of the crew." From that day on Tex was one of the best leaders we had at the plant. If they weren't doing their job, it was addressed, but it was addressed in a professional and sincere way. Easy as pie really—the Golden Rule—treat others as you want to be treated. A workable approach if ever there was one.

Unfortunately, there are many managers in every company who handle such situations poorly and create bad attitudes toward the company. It does not mean the company is bad, but it has a management challenge it needs to fix! This is the type of scenario union organizers prey and feed upon so they can make the company look bad. Isolated incidents happen in all companies, even the best-run ones.

SEIU Background

WHILE I WAS IMMERSED IN SPREADING MY WINGS IN MANAGEMENT, labor unions were still a giant part of American industry. One in particular had a rich history.

In 1921, according to the SEIU website, "members of seven janitorial unions dared to dream they could build their strength by forming a single organization, the Building Service Employees Union." Consisting of "mostly immigrant workers chartered by the AFL," and a constituency including janitors, elevator operators, and window washers, the BSEU changed its name to Service Employees International Union (SEIU) in 1968. Twelve years later, the International Jewelry Workers Union merged with SEIU with a later addition of the Drug, Hospital, and Health Care Employees Union. Based on this rich history, Chicago-based Local 1 is still organizing workers as of 2009 more than 40 years after SEIU was born.

SEIU officials boast that "during and following the Great Depression, the union was the first in the country to help other service workers, hospital caregivers and public employees unite together." This, in turn, paved "the way for the modern SEIU's three core industries: property management, public service, and health care."

To bolster signs of progress as the years passed, SEIU notes that its membership "has grown from six hundred and twenty-five thousand in 1980 to more than two million today." Key to this success, the website suggests, during a time when the majority of organized labor was shrinking, SEIU was aggressively uniting workers' strength, largely in the growing service industries. This permitted the union by the year 2000 to "become the largest and fastest growing union in North America."

SEIU members include those working in more than 100 occupations across the United States, Canada, and Puerto Rico. During its existence, it was part of the AFL–CIO umbrella organization, but winds of change began to circulate when SEIU President John Sweeney assumed command in 1995. Into the fray came a former social worker named Stern, who replaced Sweeney. By 2003, SEIU became a founding member of the "New Unity Partnership," a collection of unions seeking reform with an eye on increased union membership. Two years later, SEIU joined with other unions to form the "Change to Win Coalition," an organization bent on further reform while distancing itself from the old line AFL–CIO. When the AFL–CIO, the umbrella union, failed to listen to the SEIU and other union demands for change prior to the 2005 AFL–CIO convention, the winds of change began. The SEIU, the Change to Win Coalition, the Teamsters Union led by James Hoffa's son, and the United Food and Commercial Workers Union, disaffiliated with the AFL–CIO.

Intentions to increase membership paid off with SEIU seizing control of additional workers in Texas, Arizona, Nevada, and Florida. In Houston, more than 5,000 janitors joined the union where few had belonged before. In Florida, SEIU organized a lengthy strike at the University of Miami using strong-arm tactics including a hunger strike by employees. More than 400 janitors finally joined the union with another 600 joining from a well-known medical center in the same city. These efforts pointed to SEIU's success at recruiting low-wage sector employees, many women, minorities, and immigrants using a strategy labeled "social movement organizing." During 2006/2007, this movement would prove especially effective in Oregon where the union organized homecare workers and family-child-providers to become an effective bargaining agent with the state.

Among the most high profile of the union locals was the United Healthcare Workers East with a membership topping 250,000 and the Exotic Dancers Union in San Francisco, the only peep show/strip club local in the country. SEIU's "Justice for Janitors" campaign was memorialized in the film, *Bread and Roses*, and the character Jerry Markovic in the hit television series *ER* wore an SEIU T-shirt symbolic of the union's representation of more than a quarter million hospital service workers.

Predictably, the union has drawn its share of criticism with two websites, www.seiuexposed.com and www.unionfacts. com packed with anti-SEIU criticism. On the former, the headlines are quite bombastic: "SEIU overloads hospital emergency rooms—threatening your care at a time of need," "SEIU busts union drives of its own employees and gives millions of dollars to groups that are accused of fighting union drives," "SEIU officials sell out their member interests to boost the union's bottom line," and "SEIU bosses have been busted for political crimes accused of stealing from their own members." Portrayed above this final allegation are two hands cuffed behind a man's back.

Details provided on the "seiuexposed" website as to SEIU's business practices include information regarding union busting where employees filed suit against SEIU for the union's unfair treatment of its employer including allegations of "bullying" and forcing "an unfair contract including a demand to waive legally protected rights." Former SEIU organizer Kevin Funk was quoted: "[SEIU is] characterized by an often subtle yet convoluted net of deceit, fear-mongering, incompetence, and, in fact, union busting."

Further evidence of SEIU's destructive tendencies include the "seiuexposed" website's link between the union and the controversial community group, ACORN, which rose to prominence during the 2008 election regarding its connection to then presidential candidate Barack Obama. The website concluded ACORN actually operated two SEIU locals (880 and 100) and trained union employees to "plan and execute PR smear campaigns against SEIU-targeted companies." In 2006, the website alleged, SEIU contributed more than 2.5 million dollars to ACORN.

On its "Crime and Corruption" page, the website provides several instances of wrongdoing on the part of SEIU. Among them was an incident in Los Angeles where "SEIU members were victimized by one of the most appalling cases of union corruption in recent history," when Martin Ludlow, a city council candidate, was sentenced for "conspiracy to illegally funnel money from SEIU Local 99 to his campaign." Additional "scandals" included a June 2006 ruling by the NLRB that SEIU "interfered with the free choice of employees by illegally making promises to waive initiation fees." In California, a federal judge ruling ordered an SEIU local to pay 37,000 dollars as "punishment for failing to give members adequate information about how the union was spending employees' agency fees," and in Portland, Oregon, a disgruntled employee said "union organizers misled her co-workers by claiming that signing a union authorization card 'merely expressed her interest for a formal vote.'" Less than a year later, the website pronounced, the union agreed to suspend its "card check" organizing campaign after "employees alleged that the union relied on out-of-date cards and deceived or coerced employees into supporting the union."

Under "Terrible Tactics," the www.seiuexposed.com alleged that during "a ruthless campaign to unionize employees at two Chicago hospitals, SEIU and its 'community organization' ally at ACORN reportedly brought uninsured sick and injured people 'by the vanload' to those emergency rooms 'beyond their own communities.'" This was done, the website suggested, so "the hospital's emergency room [would be] flooded with extra patients brought in by union officials who were simply trying to make life miserable on the health care facility targeted by an organizing drive." Quoted was a Catholic Healthcare Partner's spokesman who said, "We're not opposed to unions; we're opposed to SEIU's tactics."

In Hartford, Connecticut, the website reported, SEIU's harassing attempts to cause an employer to cave in to union demands resulted in protests against the union by the very employees it was trying to organize. According to the website, complaints included "No one wants you here. You're not ever going to get voted in here. You've hurt us too much. Why would we have someone represent us who's kicked us," and "You're basically strangling our income. Why would we want to join a union that wants to choke us into submission to let you in." In California, after an alleged scam involving nursing home operators and inflated-dues paying, an SEIU member was quoted as saying, "To them, we are a huge ATM machine."

At www.unionfacts.com, the "Center for Union Facts" gathered a wealth of information about the "size, scope, political activities, and criminal activity of the labor movement in the United States of America." Defending against those who questioned its motives, the site stated it was "a non-profit organization supported by foundations, businesses, union members, and the general public. We are dedicated to showing Americans the truth about today's union leadership." To the question of "Are you against unions," the website text reads, "No. We are against union officials' abuse of power, often at the expense of their own rank-and-file members. We are against corruption, violence, and intimidation. We are against the misuse of union dues. We support employees who elect to join a union, as well as the right of employees to remain non-union without intimidation."

According to the website reports and additional information gained through various media releases, the

SEIU strategy to gather more members into its fold centered on its political agenda. The www.seiuexposed.com website suggested "to maintain its membership growth, SEIU uses its members' money to build political power. It uses that power to bully legislators and coerce business leaders and to make quid pro quo agreements with politicians that cost taxpayers millions of dollars." Perhaps the poster boy for such conduct is the scandalized former governor of Illinois, Rod Blagojevich. According to the website posting, SEIU and other strong unions supported the candidate and in return, "[He] agreed to support recognition and collective bargaining rights for both homecare and family child-care providers if he were elected governor." When this occurred, he did just that: "granting collective bargaining rights to over 20,000 personal assistants (homecare workers)."

In lockstep with the disgraced and indicted Blagojevich was Ohio Governor Ted Strickland, who, after being supported with more than a 130,000 dollar contribution from SEIU, promptly acted in the union's favor as payback. Perhaps these incidents are indicative of what SEIU President Stern meant by the comment, "We [SEIU] use the persuasion of power." If so, this power push backfired when the union was caught with its hand in the cookie jar after allegations surfaced that the union had interceded in the selection process for Obama's replacement in the Senate. According to the *Washington Post*, "Blagojevich and his chief of staff wondered aloud about a 'three-way deal' in which he would appoint Obama confidante Valerie Jarrett, a Chicago businesswoman . . . to Obama's Senate seat." In the complaint alleging the governor's wrongdoing in attempting to "sell the seat," apparently Blagojevich spoke in mid-November 2008 with "an SEIU official" based on the belief that the "official was an emissary to discuss Jarrett's interest in the Senate seat." Finally, reporter Alex MacGillis reported, Blagojevich in return would become Change to Win's executive director;

and Obama would reward Change to Win with pro-labor policies." Messy story—an unpleasant one for Stern and SEIU.

Nowhere was SEIU's quest for power more evident than during the 2008 elections. In a series of articles by *The New York Times* beginning in October 2007, the sense of strategy by Stern and SEIU became quite clear. Under the banner, "A Union With Clout Stakes Its Claims on Politics," reporter Steven Greenhouse began with the statement, "For an idea of the influence that the Service Employees International Union carries in Democratic Politics, consider that former President Bill Clinton phoned a 17-member committee of the union's New Hampshire operation last Monday to extol his wife's record on issues that are important to the labor movement." Greenhouse then noted that Clinton's "7-minute pitch" was just one indication as to how all of the Presidential candidates were "courting" the nearly two-million member union "whose financial and organizational clout are much-sought prizes, not just in the race for the White House but in Congressional and state contests."

Though Greenhouse suggested Stern had "a reputation as divisive" because he "orchestrated a split with the AFL–CIO in 2005 that some analysts say has set back labor's efforts to keep a strong voice in politics," the reporter believed Stern's "focus on politics" caused politicians to "court the SEIU endorsement aggressively." An indication of Stern's power, Greenhouse wrote, was the Democratic candidates whipping out plans for universal health care immediately after the union leader swore the union would never endorse a candidate who didn't have one, and his demand that the candidates spend a "day in the shoes of a worker." Like clockwork, Greenhouse reported, Senator John Edwards, Obama, and Hillary Clinton did so—no wonder since the SEIU had raised 40 million dollars for its political action committee in 2006, and had earmarked another 30 million for use in 2008. The money, the article suggested, would not only be used in the Presidential election but in state and local elections as well. "They are seen as huge players," Edwards' campaign manager stated, and no wonder, as Stern has said more than 100,000 volunteers could hit the streets in support of candidates of choice. With this in mind, in a veiled, or perhaps not so veiled threat, Greenhouse quoted Stern as saying, "We appreciate accountability. We just can't elect people and walk away and think it's going to work out."

Reporter Greenhouse continued his look at the influence of SEIU in a November 8, 2008 *Times* article under the banner, "After Push for Obama, Unions Seek New Rules." Priority one, the reporter concluded: "the labor unions have begun a new campaign: to get the President and Congress to pass legislation that would make it easier for workers to unionize." Noting business leaders' opposition to the strategy was Randel Johnson, Vice President for labor at the United States Chamber of Commerce. Johnson declared, "This will be Armageddon."

Greenhouse then reported, "Labor's No. 1 Priority" was "a piece of legislation called the Employee Free Choice Act" (EFCA), also known as the card-check bill. The stakes were high, Greenhouse reported that if the legislation passed, estimates were that unions could add as many as five million workers to their dues-paying list during the next five years. This would certainly increase Stern's political clout—leading straight to the oval office door.

Two sides of the fence obviously existed as to the merits of the legislation. John Sweeney, the AFL–CIO President said, "We really need a fundamental change to counterbalance corporate power and reverse the decline of the middle class," while the Chamber's Thomas Donahue believed passing the bill would be tantamount to "payback" that labor unions demanded for their backing of Obama and other candidates.

While opinions varied as to the merit of the legislation, all appeared to agree that if the bill were passed, President Obama would sign it because he was one of many co-sponsors of the bill when he was a senator. In addition, the unions had tirelessly campaigned for him while spending nearly 450 million dollars during the election. Sweeney boasted, "In the last four days of the campaign, 250,000 volunteers from AFL–CIO unions made 5.5 million phone calls and visited 3.9 million households." He estimated his volunteers "reached out to more than 13 million voters in 24 states."

Electing senators who would vote for the EFCA was important and despite 51 votes in favor, supporters could not overcome a filibuster effort by opponents where 60 votes were required. Gains by Democrats in the November election provided hope for those backing the bill especially since a Republican turned Democrat, Senator Arlen Spector, had also co-sponsored it. No matter, the man behind the legislation, SEIU President, Stern was confident that he had enough support in Congress and that the President would sign the bill. He believed it was only a matter of time before the Employee Free Choice Act would become law. Stern was one giant step from his dream of adding perhaps as many as four or five million members to SEIU's rolls. His "persuasion of power" was working its magic.

Experience That Counted

WHILE STERN WAS EARNING HIS OATS AS A LABOR UNION BOSS WITH grandiose plans, my Central Soya employment continued as the year 1982 ended. We welcomed son Mark to the family in September, 1982 despite my having been stopped for speeding two blocks from the hospital after having raced half way across Kansas trying to be there with Barb for his birth. The traffic officer felt sorry for me and just gave me a stiff warning while congratulating me on the impending arrival.

New family addition—we move! This seemed to be a pattern in our lives when Central Soya decided I needed to move a few states east to their failing Indianapolis plant. Here the challenge would be a face-to-face meeting with the Teamsters Union, one represented by guys who make Stern seem tame. This plant was a multi-purpose facility—soybean processing, edible oil, a feed mill, and a grain elevator. But the plant was in miserable shape, outdated, and in an area where no farmer in his right mind would travel to do business. Before tackling any renovations, I suggested they burn the facility down and start over as the equipment was old and the plant, filthy. The union fought me some as we tried to clean the place up, but after a rocky start, things improved a bit and we began to band together to make the facility a better place to work. Again, mutual respect was the call of the day. The employees knew what I expected— there was no tolerance for those who didn't work hard and do their jobs. In turn, I listened to union complaints with a ready eye to change things if need be. Few grievances were filed and, as time passed, peace ruled the roost.

After two years attempting to turn this plant around despite my feelings that it might best be closed, son Brian came along in May 1984. And yep, true to the new tradition, a few months later, Central Soya asked me to move again, this time to Kansas City, Missouri where morale at a new pet food facility was low and production, worse. Turn-around was the idea, but for the first time, hesitation was on my mind when Barb and I sat down and talked about pulling up stakes again, especially with three small children in tow. Kelly was in preschool and was looking at kindergarten the next year plus we were now in Indiana close to our families. After we held a meeting with the executives at Central Soya, and reasons for my request not to be transferred were heard, the proverbial "cold shoulder" came my way. By this time, the company had been purchased by Disney, yes, that's right, the mouse people, and I found their executives to be pretty matter-of-fact and less than interested in my reasons for being unwilling to leave for Missouri. The topper was when one of them said, "You're young and you're doing what you're going to be doing for the next 10 years, helping us turn plants around." I must have winced a bit at that statement, not wanting to be a vagabond my whole life while moving my kids from city to city and missing watching them grow up while working 80 hours a week. After I made it clear I wanted to stay in either Indianapolis or Fort Wayne, one of the executives said, "Well, you know, that's not really an option at this point. We want you in Kansas City. We've got problems there, we want them fixed."

Hearing this, I gathered my courage together, stood tall, and promptly resigned. On the drive home, I tried to think of a cool way to break this to Barb, but there was no cool way, so I just told her. She was a bit frantic (not sure if she threw a frying pan at me—don't believe she did), but I told her we were going to be all right and not to worry as we would find some way to feed the mouths of our three little ones. Perhaps it was my faith in God, or my faith in myself, or some faith about something, but there was no doubt in my mind that good things were going to occur. To my way of thinking, the Good Lord does watch what we are doing—what choices we are making. And when we act out of good conscience and with good intentions based on strong, inner beliefs, the old saying, "when one door closes, another one opens," does apply.

Interestingly enough, the next day a door did open when someone I had worked with at Central Soya now working at Cargill called. He had heard about my resignation and wanted to talk. I was in Minneapolis at their home office the next day, and hired as a consultant shortly thereafter. Short travels took me to their plants in Alabama and Arkansas and down to Jacksonville. Jobs at each of those locations were offered, but I just stuck to my decision to pass on any opportunity unless I could stay near my growing family back home in Indiana.

Consulting fees paid the bills and more, but when Superior Building Services, a commercial cleaning company, contacted me, I sat for an interview. There wasn't a comfortable feeling with the owner, so the job was turned down. Barb was getting a little nervous at that point and said I really needed to consider what she called "a real job." When the cleaning company owner sweetened the deal a bit with a second offer, and I became a bit more comfortable with him as a person, I decided to take a crack at working in a different industry as general manager for the state of Indiana. Learning a whole new area of business presented its problems, but over the next three-and-a-half years, I learned a great deal. Lessons learned from this kindly Jewish man included not only what the cleaning business was all about, but what being a good businessman was all about. We squabbled from time to time over management decisions because the way of doing things used at both Cargill and Central Soya had worked well for me. One example occurred on a Sunday afternoon when the owner of the company called and told me he wanted me in Cincinnati first thing on Monday morning as he had fired the general manager and that office would now be part of my territory. I inquired as to the reason for the firing and he said an account problem had popped up caused, the area manager had told him, by the general manager. When I asked whether the owner had talked to the general manager to get his side of the story and learned that he had not, I asked him to let me investigate a bit while putting the firing on hold. It turned out that a communications breakdown between the area manager, the general manager, and the customer was the culprit in addition to the need to charge more for our services. By working this problem out through discussion instead of confrontation, the general manager kept his job.

Another bone of contention was my boss's tendency to be a bit heavy-handed. This was not my way. Being strong and decisive was one thing, but going overboard with veiled threats or even unveiled threats never made much sense to me.

After three-and-a-half years working for Superior, each day the idea to try the cleaning business on my own crept more and more into my mind. Barb and I had saved some money, about 30,000 dollars as I recall, not much to some, but a great deal to others. For us, it was just enough to say, "Hey, why not take what you have learned from all the business experiences and start your own company?" The result was the birth, in May 1989, of Executive Management Services, a name that appeared appropriate because I wanted our new venture to be recognized as a multi-service company that managed building services at a professional level. Millions of people do this every year without fanfare or public notice. We were about to join them in a great risk–reward adventure.

As I scoped out the business plan and philosophy that would mark my entry into the commercial cleaning business, the family was doing well. Kelly was 8 years old and Mark, 6, with Brian in pre-school. Kelly and Mark were attending Holy Spirit Catholic School and I loved coaching their basketball and baseball teams and attending school events. Both Barb's and my parents were still living and visited us for family occasions and provided moral support. My sister Nancy was a bright, young gal who had become a registered nurse and gotten married. Barb's five brothers and sisters were involved in all different walks of life. When we gathered at Christmas, it was truly a merry time. How blessed we were!

With our savings as an investment for the future, we began our quest to own our own business. Despite having the three young ones, Barb went back to work and her law firm paycheck paid the bills and put groceries on the table. Meanwhile, my job was to locate new accounts wherever they could be found. There was a non-compete clause in my Superior resignation agreement and I honored that to the letter. Within a few months, I had picked up some small accounts. Never afraid to get my hands dirty, I cleaned my insurance company's offices, but my first real account involved a manufacturing facility that I visited, along with a banking company, at least one night a week on my way home from the office hoping to secure their business. One evening, the receptionist at the manufacturing plant front desk (I think she felt sorry for me), startled me by saying, "I've got you an appointment with the guy that oversees the contracts for the cleaning here." Next day I was sitting with the fine fellow and gave him my best pitch—what I had in mind for the company and how I could best service his facility. And he said, "Yes," causing me to nearly hug him before deciding that might not be the best idea. That evening, Barb and I celebrated, as the kids played nearby, with the knowledge that we were gaining customers who believed in my business ideals as much as I did. But money was tight and the office we found was located in a rough part of town. Certainly our first secretary learned this firsthand; while she was in the bathroom, some desperate fellow snuck through the front door and stole her coat. Later, she and I watched two gents fight to the finish outside the building. All this made me seek another home for our fledgling company.

Now that we had our first real customer, it was time to do the work. The first night on the job was memorable after I paused to look at myself in the mirror while cleaning one of the plant restrooms. Only three of the five people hired to help me had showed up and suddenly, seeing my reflection in the mirror, the thought came to me that some might say I was out of my mind having left a job where the money was good and security, a staple. But that night was special as I knew, with perseverance and hard work, the company could succeed. A vision was born and if we kept moving forward and instilled quality in all we did, the customers would come as time passed. And they did. Within a couple of months, I picked up a bank that had about 15 branches in the area. Now we were really cooking and my days became so hectic I never dared look at my watch. I just kept going and going—trying to find new clients by day, having dinner and helping Barb with payroll and the kids, and then leaving to oversee the cleaning accounts. Basketball was still in my life as a member of a pick-up team and coaching the kids' teams, something I did not want to give up.

In August, EMS won a huge account—the three Pyramids buildings on Indianapolis's north side. The size, approximately 300,000 square feet of office space, was amazing. Word was getting around, and by the end of the first year we had secured business totaling nearly a million dollars. There was no question I was spread too thin, but several people had come to work with us and soon I could delegate some of the workload so I didn't lose my sanity and my family at the same time. Barb was the rock in our life, encouraging, warning, advising, helping, encouraging again—all you could ever want in a loving wife and companion. By July 1990, she began to work with the company and a few months later, her older brother joined us as a manager to help run the operations at night while I was selling and running the business. The only downer was our learning that my mom and dad had drifted apart and were getting a divorce. And then mom had a massive stroke and passed away unexpectedly on Thanksgiving Day, 1990. A weakness she had, smoking, caught up with her and took away her life. After learning of her death, I cried, and cried, and cried some more. Hopefully she was proud of me—I owned my own business and achieved some measure of success as she hoped I would.

Such success with a small business brought with it a demanding decision for a start up like ours—the question of expansion beyond the original business plan. After much consideration we decided to gamble again, to risk again, because while my kids were continuing along in grade school enjoying learning, friendships and sports, and Barb was the best mom on the face of the earth, EMS was experiencing growing pains. This became clear when we picked up the account, National Bank of Detroit, with operations in Indianapolis and Fort Wayne. When the executives, pleased with our work after about a year, told us they were requesting bids for all of their Midwest operations, we stood up and paid attention. But I blinked when they told us the bid was an all-or-none package. Because we just wanted their Indiana business, we decided to bid on the two facilities in our home state and that was all. Then, as fast as a duck trying to evade the experienced hunter, we lost the Indiana business, a sizeable account at the time. During discussions with Barb and our small staff about what had occurred, we decided this would never happen again. If the chance arose, we would take the risk and bid for any good business we could find and start spreading our wings beyond the comfort zone. This especially made sense because, to enhance our cleaning business, we had purchased Barrett Supplies. It sold chemicals and consumable supplies like paper towels, toilet paper, hand soap, and cleaning equipment including vacuums, buffers and other supplies and equipment for the cleaning and building industry. Soon the "new" EMS had expanded to Cincinnati and Fort Wayne, and I was looking at acquiring cleaning companies in other states such as Florida, Pennsylvania, Kansas, Arizona, and New Mexico. Later we would add Superior Building Services and others to our fold, a sure sign things had come full circle from the days when I worked for them.

Along the way, true blessings continued to occur to our family and friends. As I watched from the coaching bench for the 8th grade Catholic city girls' basketball championship, Kelly hit the game winning shot at the buzzer to beat a much bigger and more talented team. Our two boys played on the same baseball team that I coached, and not only did we win the league championship, we went on to the all-star team together. We rounded up and sponsored an AAU basketball team, and coaching the boys' and girls' baseball and basketball teams was a real treat. All of our kids attended Cathedral High School. There they learned good, solid, Christian values and competitive skills we embraced. Hours spent with other Cathedral parents and families made the experience even more rewarding. Friendships are the lifeblood of special times, and preceding our move north of Indianapolis to a town called Fishers, 12 people living in our New Palestine neighborhood started a monthly euchre game where we laughed and told stories, most of them true. EMS corporate headquarters was just a few miles away, and with a few exceptions every company experiences, we never had any problems with employees. In fact, during the late 1990s when we could afford it, we started offering healthcare benefits, vacation, and holiday pay to our people and tried to push the industry along and get our customers and potential customers to buy into doing so as well. Many did. All due to that one great business acumen—treat people right and they will treat you right.

Soon my dad remarried and we enjoyed getting to know his new wife. Barb's parents also continued to do well, which was a blessing. The kids had grown up and Kelly went to Xavier University on a golf scholarship and Mark ran track at Butler; Brian ended up at my old haunt, Tri-State, to play baseball and become an engineer.

To make EMS even more of a family operation with emphasis on employee rights, Kelly joined us as marketing coordinator and within a year was promoted to human resources manager. Then Mark became interested in what we were doing and within a few months of joining the clan, he moved to Atlanta and became our business development manager. One day perhaps Brian, successful now in his own right, will show up at our office door and we will welcome him, although he is doing well in another industry close to our home. As I mentioned, even my father worked at EMS for a short time. I suspect he wanted to see if his oldest son really knew what he was doing.

Over time, the success EMS has enjoyed has touched the lives of many people. From the day when Barb threw her love and support behind me when we decided to take the journey that led to happiness and joy in so many ways as the year 2006 appeared on the horizon, we had fought together to establish a first-rate company with a reputation for excellence like few in its field. And then, like a vulture out of the sky, Stern and his SEIU cohorts swooped down and threatened us with destruction if we did not bow to their commands. Soon Stern and I would be at loggerheads as I faced the biggest challenge of my life.

Persuasion of Power

"SEIU PRESIDENT ANDY STERN IS THE DRAMA QUEEN OF BIG LABOR."

This rather unflattering depiction of Stern appeared in a July 2008 *Wall Street Journal* (WSJ) article. It reported, "The Service Employees International Union is staging nationwide rallies this week to 'Take Back the Economy' from wealthy private equity firms. Based on the evidence of pension policies, however, SEIU members would do better to take back their own pensions from union chieftains."

Before examining the WSJ's allegations, it is important to understand who Stern is. And why he targeted EMS as a plum operation to be unionized at all cost.

According to his 2006 book, *A Country That Works*, Stern "was born to white-collar, professional parents in a community where unions were rarely mentioned." Further, Stern said, "I went to an Ivy League college and never held a union job until I started working as a social worker in 1972." He noted having expected to become an attorney, but instead, after college, sold newspapers on street corners in Massachusetts, administered tests to census workers, and became a substitute teacher at Benjamin Franklin High School in Philadelphia.

In his book, Stern wrote, "Reflecting on my life, I realize that the seeds of my commitment to dignity of work, and to organizations that give hope, voice, and strength to ordinary hardworking people, were planted in my upbringing." This commitment, he added, was best understood in an "ethical will" he wrote during some religious training. There he imagined "a world of concentric and cross-influencing circles; at the core of the innermost circle was the individual, grounded by principled action and an ethical life." Surrounding each individual, he decided, were the "concentric circles of family, community, and nation, each influencing the next." His directive in the will was to urge "friends and family to 'state what you believe in and reach for higher standards that you have already attained.'" These principles, he said, "guide my actions to this day, and more important, are the basis for a country that works."

Stern believed that his mother, a college graduate with honors who had given up any sense of a career to raise him and his two brothers, and his father, a lawyer for family-owned businesses who had worked his way through college waiting tables after losing his father when he was only 13, were the illuminating forces in his life. Growing up on "The Hill" in West Orange, New Jersey, where neighbors were "mostly white-collar workers, some Jewish, some not," Stern attended an elementary school where no religious, job status, or wealth separations among the students existed. Ironically, the future labor leader's bar mitzvah in Newark was earmarked for November 22, 1963, the very day when President John F. Kennedy was assassinated.

Stern wrote that his first exposure to "organized protest" occurred upon his arrival at the University of Pennsylvania's Wharton School of Business. First, he joined fellow students protesting the requirement to wear a tie at meals, and then participated in the attempt to prevent the university from building a parking lot in an area of open green space. Perhaps he should have spent more time in the classroom, Stern admitted, because when he graduated in 1971, he had gained the dubious distinction of "having attended the least number of classes in Penn's undergraduate history."

From Penn, it was on to Europe before "wandering aimlessly around New England," and working at various jobs in Philadelphia. He then accepted a civil-service position at the Vine District Welfare Office, which, he admitted, "led to the start of my union career." Here occurred a milestone with Stern writing, "The story of my official entry into the union is rather anticlimactic. Despite its accidental nature, it marked the moment when my lifelong passion for the labor movement was born." This caused him to realize, he said, that "the union heritage of fighting for social and economic justice and being on the side of the powerless touched within me a deep-seated belief in equity and community that has never faded."

The defining moment occurred, Stern contended, when he attended a Vine Street lunchtime meeting of the Pennsylvania Social Service Union (PSSU), a chartered affiliate of SEIU. It represented more than 10,000 white-collar workers employed in the state's welfare and social service agencies.

At the luncheon, after seizing on the opportunity to eat as much free pizza as possible, the 23-year-old listened with interest as various union matters were discussed. When it was time to elect an assistant shop steward, a staff representative, according to Stern's version of the story, walked over to him, and even though he didn't know him, asked his name. Seconds later, with the smell of pepperoni pizza in the air, the shop steward called out Stern's name as a nominee, and presto, he was unanimously elected.

Soon, Stern admitted in his book, he "fell in love with union life" while attending meetings around Pennsylvania as he pursued a law degree at Temple University's night school. Soon he was standing on the picket lines protesting a worthy cause, with an early impression of his suspicions that the "structure of the union provided the staff with disproportionate authority for decision making, as opposed to the more democratic empowerment of the members that I thought was in the true spirit of the labor movement." Disproportionate authority seemed to conveniently escape Stern as he rose to power in the SEIU! Ready to assume a more prominent role, he became a full-time field representative for the union's Philadelphia chapter. This led to his running for President of the local union. Not only did he win, but married his "election partner," Jane, as the year turned to 1983. Flush with ideas for change, Stern then transformed the local SEIU affiliate into "a more modern, innovative, and aggressive organization."

During his days in Pennsylvania, Stern said he learned two fundamental lessons: 1) "unions allow the powerless to unite their strength and become more powerful," and 2) "the ways in which unions were structured and doing business had to change." This was because there was no doubt, Stern wrote, "the failure of American labor laws to adequately protect workers' rights is a stain on our democracy." This, he said, was due to the establishment of "statutory amendments" weakening the true intention, the guts, of the National Labor Relations Act (NLRA). Among other provisions, the NLRA had initially provided for union cards signed by employees to be used in deciding whether a union could organize at a particular employer. This procedure had been washed away through the years, Stern said, and the NLRA election procedure, one utilizing the secret-ballot method, had become, in his view, a "frustrating process for workers and a litigation nightmare." He believed management and its lawyers were the culprits because their delaying tactics could prevent elections for more than a year during which time "indirect threats could be made to employees, as well as blatant intimidation," with some leading to dismissal of union-oriented employees. Because employers were not subject to any punitive damages for such actions, the fired employees had "no real-world remedies." This caused the SEIU, even thought it was the seventh largest union in the country, to lack, in Stern's opinion, "a public profile," and to be "disparagingly referred to as "SEIU who?"

According to Stern, for the next 12 years, he led the charge for reform with the support of SEIU's President, John Sweeney. Using new tactics, including recruiting organizers from rival unions, the union flourished and within eight years, SEIU doubled the membership numbers. Key to the increases was the Justice for Janitors Campaign, the Dignity, Rights, and Respect Campaign relating to nursing home workers, and the We're Worth It! Campaign for public-sector employees. Stern believed the soul of the union was the janitorial workers and noted that in nearly all of the janitors' unions, membership had severely declined. One reason, he decided, was because "cleaning was no longer provided by the building owners but was contracted out to cleaning companies, which were becoming larger and more sophisticated." These companies, Stern suggested in his book, "were gaining market share, yet they had no allegiance to long-standing local union relationships," an indication Stern had companies like ours in his sights even before he became SEIU's national President.

What was the remedy, according to Stern? After listening to union employers cry about being unable to compete with non-union companies because they had to pay union wages and benefits while non-union employers didn't providing an unfair competitive advantage to the non-union employers, he realized a simple strategy was necessary: "Our priority should not be to make unionized employers noncompetitive by raising the wages and benefits they offered their employees over the non-union company's wages in the market. Instead, our priority should be to *contribute* to our employers' success by organizing *all* their competitors."

If this was accomplished, apparently whether the particular company provided better wages and benefits than the union norm or not, Stern believed, "Only then would we be able to bargain contracts that set the same minimum standards for all the competing employers and thus take wage differentials off the table." Patting himself on the back, Stern wrote, "We thought the theory brilliant, a win-win situation."

Despite the brilliance, Stern recognized two challenges: 1) building relationships with employers where value [more productivity] was a plus for them despite padding employee paychecks, and 2) means by which workers could "make free and fair choices about union representation without shedding blood at their workplaces." The key: "The former required the power of persuasion and the latter the persuasion of power." The agenda: "Although we preferred to lead with the power of persuasion, with many resistant employers we were often left no choice but to use the persuasion of power." Apparently, based on what was about to occur, EMS and I fit into the latter category.

To implement his strategy on a personal basis, Stern needed a bully pulpit. This became possible after he had worked under Sweeney at the national SEIU headquarters as organizing director. When Sweeney resigned to become President of the AFL–CIO, SEIU Secretary-Treasure Dick Cordtz was the anointed successor. Disappointed with Cordtz's intent to follow old-line policies, Stern decided to challenge him. Upset with the absence of loyalty, Cordtz fired Stern but then lost to him in a 1996 election. Stern now headed the SEIU, a long journey from the day when he had been surprised to become an assistant shop steward to the local SEIU chapter. In his book, Stern noted, "It's my job to watch out for the threats that confront our members— and all American workers—and to find solutions to improve their lives."

Stern's first move in that direction caused him to concentrate on "organizing strategically for growth." Over the next 10 years, he would do just that and by 2005, more than two million members belonged to SEIU. Hard work, and dedication to improving the plight of the common man and woman, had paid off. At least that is what Stern, my future adversary, preached.

Others had a differing view. In January 2005, *The New York Times Magazine* profiled Stern under the subtitle, "The New Boss." Reporter Matt Bai began the article by writing, "Purple is the color of Andrew Stern's life. He wears, almost exclusively, purple shirts, purple jackets, and purple caps. He carries a purple duffel bag and drinks bottled water with a purple label, emblazoned with the purple logo of the Service Employees International Union, of which Stern is President." Later, Bai added a vivid description of the-then 54-year-old Stern: "He is a lean, compact man with thinning white hair, and when he reclines in the purple chair in his Washington office and crosses one leg over the other, he could easily pass for a psychiatrist or a math professor."

When Stern had attempted to disconnect his nearly two million workers and what amounted to a 6.5 billion dollar enterprise from the AFL–CIO, the tactic did not endear him to other union leaders. In the article, Tom Buffenbarger, President of the union that represented machines and aerospace workers, told Bai, "What Andy's doing now with his compadres is what Vladimir Putin is trying to do to the Communist bloc countries. He's trying to implement dictatorial rule." Later in the article, Buffenbarger called Stern "an arrogant usurper" and compared him to "a rather small peacock." He then said Stern was "enamored of all the glitz and hype of Wall Street types. He must be a fan of Donald Trump. I think he wants his own TV show." Reading Buffenbarger, it would lead you to believe that Stern is a legend in his own mind.

Former boss John Sweeney was tough on Stern as well based on accusations that Stern's grand ideas for revolutionizing the union movement "incited fury within a lot of smaller unions, whose members don't seem to think the movement needs a self-appointed savior." "Andy is impatient," Sweeney said, "I think he needs to stand still for a minute and listen to what other people think." In a telling point to this and other characterizations based on the financial fiascos during the 2008/2009 economic downturn, Stern suggested that unions merge into global unions even though the smaller ones resented it, "What was good for GM ended up being good for the country." Later, when GM was on the verge of bankruptcy, he would change this tune as a guest on the Charlie Rose television program.

In an update to Stern's plans, *The New York Times* reporter Steven Greenhouse chronicled some bumps in the road in early 2008. In an article titled, "Union Grows, but Leader Faces Criticism," the reporter displayed the comments of Sal Rosselli, President of one of SEIU's largest locals with representation of more than 140,000 California health care workers. His view: ". . . an overly zealous focus on growth—growth at any cost, apparently—has eclipsed SEIU's commitment to its members." Later, in April, the *Times* reported "Poor Andy Stern," before documenting his failed attempt to organize private equity firms that "even his fellow labor leaders seem to think is a bad idea." Such an agenda caused the *Times* to suggest his real goal "was expanding his own political clout," but Stern denied any aspirations for a personal role in politics with carefully chosen words that left the door open to seeking office in the future.

Such depictions did not add to the superior image Stern wished to portray, and an incident in Oakland, California during this time pointed fingers at how rough and tough Stern, and the SEIU organizers, had become. This was clear based on a district court issuing a restraining order against Stern and the SEIU over allegations "that SEIU members stalked, harassed, and physically assaulted members of the California Nurses Association."

These incidents, and others, had caused the *Wall Street Journal* in July 2008 to refer to Stern as the "the drama queen of Big Labor," one who "wants to pound [equity] firms with bad publicity and political retribution until they break." While we did not own an equity firm, we would learn how true the allegations against Stern and SEIU were. He was about to attack with his Corporate Campaign against EMS as well as any one else who stood in his way, and with a viciousness that I could have never predicted in my wildest dreams.

Learning about Stern was illuminating, especially since the realization hit me that he had never worked for any companies for a significant period of time, and for certain, never had owned a business of any kind. This caused me to question how he could relate at all to blue-collar workers like those he sought to organize as he had never stood in their shoes day after day, month after month, and year after year while they earned a living to support their families. And there was no doubt of his inability to relate to business owners like me who put their money at risk, fought hard to start a business, fought harder to make it grow, and even harder still to sustain that business by making payroll every week in a marketplace fluctuating on a daily basis. Stern thus had no practical, firsthand experience in the real world with employer–employee relationships as he had never been in the trenches dealing with such matters. Through my career dealings with numerous personality types, Stern appeared to me to be the prototypical individual who could not make it in the private sector through his own talents of persuasion, but learned how confrontation and intimidation via the union could make him successful and allow him to achieve his goals by forcing his will on others or in his own words "persuasion of power." But none of this apparently made any difference to Stern: he believed EMS had to be unionized and that was that. Armed with this combative mindset, he and SEIU were ready to engage me in a battle that would test our strength like Roman gladiators fighting to save being thrown to the lions.

Employees: The Greatest Asset

LABOR UNION INNOVATOR SAMUEL GOMPERS ONCE SAID, "THE ENEMY of the worker is an unprofitable employer." I couldn't agree more, and the key part of becoming profitable is how the employer treats employees. Without them, especially those on the front lines doing the unglamorous work, companies like EMS could fail and jobs would be lost.

If Stern and his SEIU organizers had done their homework, had taken the time to visit our corporate offices, the buildings and plants we serviced, and spoken to any number of our thousands of employees, blue- and white-collar, here is what they would have discovered—a vibrant, exciting, well-managed company with a strong focus on rigid employee hiring methods, better-than-industry average wages and health care benefits, clean working environments, and a willingness to go the extra mile to protect employees from any harm whether it was harassment, threat, or simply the right to exercise freedom at the ballot box if and when unionization became an issue.

Doesn't sound too bad, right? Because we had started with nothing, not one customer in 1989, and now had thousands in 30-some states with an employee roll of close to 5,000, then we must have done something right. Even the briefest research would have told Stern and his union buddies "Hey, EMS seems to be running a good ship, one where they treat the employees with the kind of respect we admire. Maybe we should use EMS as a model company for how other companies should treat their employees. Otherwise, let's leave them alone because the employees are doing just fine." But this mindset was not to be, and instead Stern and the union rushed in with a "do it our way or else" mentality in tandem with their threat that the "persuasion of power" shall prevail. When someone does this, as the union did with EMS, then the war was on, one I did not ask for and did not want, but could not avoid.

In fact, if Dennis Dingow, the SEIU's front-line contract manager, or Stern would have asked, I could have given them inspiring employee stories to fill a notebook. We were especially proud of how many employees had started with us and then built a career as they moved to positions with more responsibility. And that notebook could also be filled with instances where we protected the employees from those who treated them as second-class citizens, something we never tolerated. Pick on one of my employees, and you pick on me, and every other EMS employee, and together, we will come after you. I have long believed that good management not only means providing good jobs in a safe environment for fair pay, but also ensuring my employees' rights are effectively protected.

Inspiring employee stories at EMS abound. One particular gentleman named Mark, an impressive, good-looking guy with a quick mind, owned a little boat repair business, but he worked for us part-time cleaning bank branches. He liked what he was doing and wanted to do more. Soon he had worked his way up to being a supervisor before eventually attaining a salaried site manager's position at one of our larger buildings. From there, he leaped into the sales area, and after working there for a while, decided to leave for Florida, his home state, where he worked for a contract cleaning company. When the fellow he was working for decided to retire, our former employee called us and asked if we wanted to buy the company. We did, and Mark became our Tampa general manager. He worked for us a while, but when we had to replace him, I wondered who might be qualified to take over. While visiting the office, Mark's secretary, a spirited woman with a bit of managerial experience, had impressed me. I called her in the office and asked her if she thought she could be a general manager. Based on her positive answer and willingness to work hard, we hired her on the spot.

Another employee, a Hispanic man named George, started working for us as an hourly cleaner in an Indianapolis church. He was promoted to supervisor there and then to site manager for a large private school we cleaned. But he wanted more, and soon we moved him to Ft. Myers, Florida to run a small branch in that area where he flourished.

On the management side of the business, a general manager at Maple Creek Country Club decided he wanted a change of scenery. We hired him to join us at EMS as an operations manager. He worked his way through our company and became one of our Executive Vice Presidents. In another part of the country, when we made an acquisition a few years ago in the Wichita, Kansas area, we discovered management needed to be strengthened. But they had a controller I liked; a good people person, and we quickly moved him into the branch manager's position while the woman who was the branch manager switched to sales. We try very hard to match people to their skills and abilities, something we try to accomplish with every employee position whether it is supervising a building operation or cleaning the offices. My philosophy is that it is much like a sports team. In baseball you wouldn't put a person who is best suited as a catcher in center field or vice versa. Why then wouldn't you use the same philosophy in business? Seems like common sense to me, but it alludes many people!

This was especially true for a fellow who came to work at EMS almost 20 years ago. He had his heart set on becoming an operations manager, but I told him sales might be a better position for him. He was leery of my recommendation, but he took the job and became my first salesman. He was in outside sales for a year before becoming a sales manager with a couple of people working for him. Now he's our Vice President of sales managing a fairly large sales force. There are many more stories like this since we have seen many people start with us in one position and move to others or begin to work for EMS as part-time help, eventually moving into managerial or supervisory positions. These people have been with EMS a long time, and they are the heart and soul of the company.

Plain and simple, we don't really tout the business at EMS; we tout the employees. Any customer letters of commendation received are reprinted in the company newsletters. I also send a signed personal letter and a Wal-Mart gift certificate to every employee who is praised. Employees of the month and the year are honored, with the latter receiving a plaque, other gifts, and a nice bonus. The runners-up receive a gift certificate. All this is part of our appreciation for a job well done.

Another step we have taken to help employees make it through tough economic times is to implement a nationwide purchasing program so that our employees at all levels receive discounts at different retail stores. These include Costco, Target, Lenovo, Office Depot, Avis, Seaworld, and Disneyworld. Soon employees may shop online.

Protecting employees, as Stern and SEIU would have learned if they had just checked out our record, is standard operating procedure at EMS and our doing so has paid off through employee advancement and loyalty. As we've grown through the years, there have been instances where I've canceled business because our employees were being mistreated. One instance occurred at a large Indianapolis office building with a property manager who was difficult at best. He continued to howl over his belief that our employees were leaving doors unlocked at a facility where his company employees were working around the clock. The woman in charge of our operation told him our employees left at midnight and thus had no control over what occurred in the building after they left. But he called me and complained while demanding I see him immediately along with our EMS manager. When we arrived in his office, he began his tirade by swearing and using the F word, and without hesitation, I told him "Stop using that kind of language when a lady is in the room." He looked at me like I was crazy and started ranting again, using language even more foul than before. I stopped him in mid-sentence, stood up, and said "This meeting is over. I'm not going to have my manager subjected to this type of behavior." We left and when I arrived back at our corporate offices, I dictated a termination letter and faxed it down to the property manager. The result: we had just lost a several-hundred-thousand-dollar-a-year account. No matter, to me, the larger issue, the only issue, was taking care of employees so they were never subjected to abuse.

From time to time, I've canceled several accounts with customers like that where there were instances of abuse or hostility toward our employees, our management team, or even clerical people they talk to in the office. I've coached our sales representatives and business development managers to understand that if they call on someone and they seem difficult to deal with, pass on the account because if they are difficult with sales people, they will be difficult with our cleaning staff. We don't want to be involved in relationships that compromise EMS core values.

What do we look for in employees? Since we built EMS from the ground up based on five characteristics precious to me—hard work, honesty, integrity, skill level, and perseverance—these are essential qualities we strive to find in anyone interested in working with us. I want people who believe in themselves, are willing to work hard hour after hour and day after day, and are not going to give up when times get tough because there will be obstacles along the way like the ones we faced when EMS was just an infant. Bottom line—I just want good people.

Because nearly 90 percent of start-ups like ours fail, it is important to recognize a common thread among those that make it—the competitive nature of the core management group. I believe my athletic competitiveness helped me with that area because I hate to lose whether it is at tiddlywinks, on the golf course, or when we are bidding for a contract. Failure is acceptable, but only if you have given it your all, and then about 25 percent more than that. And if I am willing to give this type of effort, I want employees who will do the same whether they are management or hourly-wage earners.

As a result of EMS's success, several offers to purchase the company have been tendered through the years, but my love affair with this family-owned business operated with employee fairness prevents me from selling. Because of our growth, I don't know as many of the employees today as I used to years ago. But I still visit with as many as possible and introduce myself and tell them how pleased we are they work for us. Sometimes I even wish I were on the firing line again cleaning offices. One great memory that makes me grin when I think about it occurred with some of our women employees, many of whom were quite short. I knew they had trouble dusting in high places and when they saw me coming, they knew I was going to check to see if they had cleaned there. After a time, when I visited, the women would escort me to the high places and show me that somehow they had figured out a way to get the job done. It was almost like a game and we had fun with it. Their willingness to go the extra mile to make EMS look good caused me to make certain they were treated well.

When we buy a company, the first thing we do is to evaluate the management personnel to make certain they are in tune with our core business values and culture. If they are not, we replace them with people who are, ones who will watch out for our hourly employees. Certainly, we give people a chance to fit into our culture, and people do change their habits for the good, but we want to make certain that those who work for us will make good decisions regarding workers who decide that EMS is the right place for them.

Perhaps if Stern or Dennis Dingow had requested to visit EMS headquarters, or spoken with me at length, they would have discovered that yes, my spiritual foundation as a Catholic does impact my management style. But religion is a private matter and we don't blow our beliefs into other people's faces despite our attending weekly mass where we visit with the priest we know well. Without a spiritual foundation to guide them, I am not certain how people evaluate their conduct, and being Catholic has permitted me to do so, to ask whether this decision or that is in line with my beliefs. Prayer is also special to me as I ask for guidance to do what is best for my family and business because, let's face it, we are normally right about half the time, if that. If we were perfect, the world would be a better place, but this is not possible with all the temptations lurking at every turn. This is especially true concerning the greed and power that has gripped so many in the business world, people like Bernard Madoff and others who had blatantly stolen from business associates, friends, and even family.

During a chat Stern and I might have had, one thing would have become crystal clear—I love EMS. And I become quite emotional talking about it because I am quite an emotional person. At dinners and special events, sometimes these emotions get the best of me and I have to stop for a minute to gather my composure. As the year 2006 began, I was just so damn proud of what we had accomplished with employees living all around the country. When the first contact from Dennis Dingow occurred, I promised myself that no one was going to push us around, and no one was for certain going to abuse our employees because if this occurred, I could never look at myself in the mirror again.

Employee Free Choice Act (EFCA) / Union Power Grab

THE TORNADO I WAS ABOUT TO TACKLE BY RESISTING THE SEIU's attempts to unionize EMS was about one thing, and one thing only—Stern's desire to unionize every company in my industry. But at the epicenter of his grandiose plan was a piece of legislation called, as briefly mentioned before, The Employee Free Choice Act (EFCA), a misnomer if there ever was one. Give those folks at SEIU credit; the wording is brilliant, and the plan to gain passage of the legislation even more innovative. These are bright people with an agenda they truly believe is worthy. I simply disagree.

What is the EFCA? Simply put, it is a proposed law that would change existing federal law concerning the rights of workers to unionize. Instead of unions like the SEIU arriving at the doorstep of companies like mine with a petition for a secret-ballot election to be held under the auspices of the NLRB, or demand I sign a "Neutrality Agreement," (in essence, submit to card check), the legislation would guarantee EMS would be subject to card check recognition. If EFCA passes, employees seeking union representation would indicate their willingness to do so by signing union cards authorizing such representation. In addition, there would also be severe penalties assessed against employers that violate employee rights concerning union establishment, and new mediation and binding arbitration procedures for any first-contract disputes.

The legislation was initially filed in the 108th Congress and during the 110th Congress under H. R. 800. In March 2007, the House of Representatives passed the bill, originally introduced by Representative George Miller (D-California). The vote was 241–185 mostly along political party lines. The House Majority Leader Steny Hoyer (D-Maryland) said the bill was about "establishing fairness in the workplace," while his counterpart, Minority Leader John Boehner (R-Ohio) believed the true purpose was to "take care of union bosses." How many representatives actually read the bill is unknown, but if the 2008 Stimulus Bill is any indication, one has to wonder who among the representatives really understood its content and potential impact as any bill with wording including "Free Choice" sounds good at first glance.

At the foundation of the bill is the card check provision. While current law permits those seeking union representation to demand an election from employers utilizing a "secret ballot" procedure akin to any local, state, or national election, in reality a "private ballot" election, the new law forces the "card check" procedure noted above. Under this procedure, a union would be certified as the exclusive bargaining representative of the employees as soon as it submits signatures from a bare majority of workers. While authorization cards are used today to show a minimum level of support for the government to conduct an election, an election provides important safeguards that allow workers to cast their vote in private. Card check eliminates these safeguards. The employee's decision to sign or not sign an authorization card will be known to union organizers, co-workers, and the employer. Simply put, if the law passes, co-workers would know how each person voted, wiping privacy out of the equation. Additionally, all size businesses would be targeted from mom and pops to major corporations. Theoretically, a business owner could leave on Friday and return to work on Monday and be presented with notification that they would be required to recognize a particular union, and they would never would have a clue what was transpiring.

Regarding "first contract mediation and arbitration procedures," the proposed legislation permits either the union or management engaged in first contract negotiation to forward any dispute to the Federal Mediation and Conciliation Service (FMCS) after 90 days have passed. If mediation does not bring the parties to agreement after a 30-day time period, binding arbitration is the next step with any decision final without legal recourse for two years with extensions possible if the parties agreed. Interest arbitration would set every term and condition of the union contract. This would not be limited to wages and benefits, but work rules, contracting, management rights, and every other provision that typically is included in a union contract. There is no requirement that the arbitrator's decision be consistent with the employer's business model and the employees have no voice and no vote as to whether the arbitrator's contract is in their best interest.

To provide a hammer toward management being cooperative regarding potential unionization, EFCA would invoke more severe penalties for any employer violations during the unionization process. These include fines in an amount up to twenty thousand dollars for any one violation where management willfully or repeatedly violates the employees' rights during any unionization campaign or the first contract period. When proof exists that any employee is discharged unlawfully as payback for attempting to unionize, or there is discrimination in any form during either the unionization or first contract period, a "three times back pay" provision is instituted meaning back wages would be tripled inflicting what amounts to punitive damages against the employer. What is disconcerting about this is the potential for unions to file frivolous unfair labor practices in droves hoping some will stick, causing the company to endure undue financial hardship defending the charges while being reluctant to talk to employees while the charges are pending. Notably, the bill lacks similar penalties for union misconduct, allowing unions to get away with practices that would result in substantial penalties if engaged in by employers.

With all that was at stake for both employers and the unions, hot debate was expected, and occurred. Those favoring the bill believed it was a protection device for workers, pointing out that under current law weeks or even months might pass before an election was held with the delay discouraging those seeking unionization. In fact, the NLRB is required by its own regulations to conduct union elections within 42 days of a petition being filed—a standard the board routinely follows in administrating elections.

Pro-EFCA backers also support the bill by saying it really does not change the law, it just shifts the choice of card check recognition from the employer to the employee. This is laughable on two fronts. First, the employer would never voluntarily agree to card check unless it was pounded into submission by a union to sign a Neutrality Agreement, and second, it is even more absurd to suggest that the employees would make the choice. The unions, not the employees, are the masterminds of organizing drives, and the unions will never choose to submit to a secret ballot election when they have the option to secure recognition through card check rather than submitting to a secret ballot procedure. Moreover the card check process heavily favors unions because employees can be easily pressured into signing cards, at work, at their homes, or other places away from work, and in environments (such as the local wings and beer joint) in which the employer has no opportunity to present its position as to why a union is not in the employees' best interest! In the card check scenario, the union will never keep the employees informed and will harass and intimidate the rest of the employees until they achieve the coveted bare majority!

The pro-EFCA folks also claim that employers threaten and intimidate workers to prevent them from siding with union organizers, or that employers tell inflated stories of the horrors of unionization designed to scare employees away from unions they would otherwise support. In addition, they claim that existing law provides insufficient protection to employees from the actions of unscrupulous employers. They claim that these employers will discharge an employee they find to support the union, simply in an effort to keep the union out of their workplace. The reality, however, is quite the opposite. In the majority of cases, employers can show that employees were disciplined or discharged for legitimate reasons unrelated to union organizing. In those cases in which wrongful actions do happen, the National Labor Relations Board vigilantly seeks reinstatement of those workers, including the ordering of back pay, such that the employee is made whole. However, unions like to quote inaccurate figures to justify their cause to the naive public and politicians.

The unions point to all the NLRB charges filed over the years against employers as evidence of the terrible things companies do to their employees. What they fail to tell you is, that in most cases, it is the unions who file the claims (not the employees); the majority of claims are frivolous and designed to force the company to cave under union pressure. Amazingly, the SEIU filed more than three dozen unfair labor practices against EMS during the course of its three-year campaign against my company, including more than a dozen charges that EMS had discriminated against employees based upon their union activities by disciplining them, withholding their paychecks, or even firing them without good reason. Do you know how many of those discrimination charges were found to have merit by the National Labor Relations Board? Not a single one! Zero.

Finally, I heard on the radio a labor union attorney say that despite the fact that companies claim that unions are the ones doing the harassing, a study done by a Human Resources company indicated that there were only 40 to 100 charges against unions for harassment against employees over the past 10 years or so. Why is that? First, because employees either don't know they can go to the NLRB and file a report or they are afraid to because of union retaliation; second, employers tend not to file as many frivolous charges as unions; and third, statistics are used deceptively as described next.

Organized labor cites a statistic from the National Labor Relations Board that more than 31,358 employees received back pay awards from employers. This statistic is misleading, however, and in no way indicates the number of employees discriminated by or coerced by employers during organizing drives. Indeed, the vast majority of back pay awards (25,620) were the result of informal settlement where no finding of coercion exists at all. In addition, the numbers are not broken down to indicate how many were due to unlawful coercion during organizing and how many represent other violations of the act, such as unlawful discharge after a union contract is in place. In other words, the statistics relied on by the unions are not confined to coercive employer practices during organizing drives or before first contracts are reached and are not indicative of a finding (or even an allegation) of employer coercion at all.

Conversely, in support of the position that there are very few instances in which unions have been found to have harassed or intimidated employees, unions rely upon a skewed AFL–CIO review of cases identified by the HR Policy Association in previous Congressional testimony. The HR Policy Association (then called LPA, the Labor Policy Association) testimony was related to the loose rules governing the authorization card process. It cited *as examples*, not as a definitive count, a number of cases in which union coercion was present in the signing of authorization cards. The AFL–CIO review of those cases found 42 that they agreed involved coercion. Labor unions and their allies now refer to this as the definitive number of cases finding union coercion in the organizing process—a number deceptively determined by the unions themselves!

Hard data comparing actual employer coercion and union coercion during an organizing drive and before a first contract is reached is difficult to attain. While not at all conclusive, looking at allegations of coercive behavior provides some insight. For example, the NLRB reports that in fiscal year 2005 there were 8,047 charges of employer discrimination or illegal discharge, while there were 5,405 charges of union coercion and illegal restraint in addition to another 594 cases of union discrimination. These numbers are clearly not completely satisfactory because they are allegations only, and do not account for the fact that unions are likely to file more frivolous charges than employers, and because they are not narrow enough to be confined to organizing drives and the time period before a first contract is reached. One thing is clear, however—the numbers are not so lopsided as organized labor and their allies would have you believe—thousands of cases of union intimidation as well as employer intimidation are filed every year.

I believe we should all agree that intimidation by employers as well as intimidation by union organizers is wrong. While our nation's labor laws may not be perfect, at least they provide a federally-supervised process by which a worker can privately make the important decision about whether to join a union, without his or her employer, co-workers, or union organizers knowing how he or she ultimately voted. We should be working to strengthen workers' privacy rights in making this important decision, not effectively eliminating them. Furthermore, I consider myself a patriot and would like to stress again I am not anti-union, but I am against organizing tactics such as Corporate Campaigns, that bully people or companies into submission, or bills like EFCA aimed at circumventing current law or time honored American traditions such as the secret ballot election. In this respect I will always stand up for individual liberties and the free market system!

Labor union support for the legislation is almost universal. **(The Fraternal Order of Police oppose EFCA. Kudos to them!)** During the House hearings in 2007, union leaders suggested reform was long overdue based on the diminishing status of those people classified as "working class" citizens. They pointed to wage discrepancies, health care neglect, poor working conditions, and the widening gap between the rich and the poor. This was occurring, they argued, while corporate profits were at an all-time high during 2007/2008 when debacles such as Citibank and AIG had not lost billions of dollars.

Through significant increases in unification, supporters of EFCA said collective bargaining could narrow this gap while providing more individual opportunity and economic stability toward the middle class. They boasted that union workers on the whole earned at least 30 percent more than non-union workers with those numbers increasing among African-Americans, Latinos, and women. Health care, union advocates also noted, was better handled at lower cost at unionized companies while pension benefits were more secure for those who considered retirement. Above all, EFCA advocates believed the new law would assist the plight of low-wage earners, including janitors, cooks, cashiers, childcare and nursing home caregivers through elimination of the secret-ballot elections as unionization would be more possible than before. Based on our experience with the SEIU's contracts, this seemed very unlikely, but those in favor of the EFCA believed they were right and I respected their opinions, as I asked them to respect mine.

During debate on the House bill, the AFL–CIO released polls indicating than more than 75 percent of the American people believed in worker freedom regarding the decision to unionize or not. Just as many, they said, were in favor of making it easier for employees to become organized. The polls did not say, however, that Americans were in favor of eliminating the secret ballot election. In fact, the majority of Americans were against such a proposal.

Those opposing the EFCA bill were just as strenuous in their belief that the current NLRB rules were the best means by which to ensure not only choice, but freedom of choice as "secret" or "private" balloting permitted those who voted anonymously to be guaranteed no chance of repercussion regardless of how they voted. Confidentiality, they argued, was the American way, a safeguard important to making certain that free choice and free will pervaded. Pressure, coercion, misrepresentation, deceit, threat, and harassment, they believed, disappeared from the equation when employees could vote their conscience with no threat they might be scorned by fellow workers, physically and/or mentally abused, or even ridiculed based on their beliefs. Perhaps it was Republican Representative John Kline who summed up legislation opponents' viewpoint best: ". . . How can one possibly claim that a system whereby everyone— your employer, your union organizer, and your co-workers— knows exactly how you vote on the issue of unionization gives an employee 'free choice' . . . I cannot fathom how we can . . . take away a worker's democratic right to vote in a secret-ballot election and call it 'Employee Free Choice.'"

Kline and others opposing the bill also disagreed with the "card check" provision where workers could be influenced by union propaganda and pressure because of the lack of provision for union fines. Management's side of the story would also be prohibited from view because they could not speak to employees about the union's organizational campaign for fear of onerous fines for frivolous unfair labor practice charges—essentially, a gag order on the company. As for the binding arbitration provision, it was the "word" binding that opponents of the bill wrestled with because the final solution to any management/union dispute would be left in the hands of an arbitrator, one appointed by the government with little industry experience, to decide with no future recourse for either party. But the unions favor this provision as there is an automatic two-year contract in place and better still, immediate revenue from union dues.

Voices objecting to the EFCA pointed to incidents like the one in 2007 in Minnesota where a daycare worker targeted by SEIU told of being manipulated into signing cards simply so the union could give them additional information about the union. The woman felt as if she was tricked because, in reality, signing the card meant she was voting for unionizing the company she worked for. Her comment: "Their agenda is to gain money for themselves, not better the child-care industry. . . ." Perhaps money is a true objective as the top ten executives at SEIU earn total salaries that are just a few bucks shy of *two million dollars*, with Stern leading the way with an annual salary of more than a quarter million. One also has to wonder who paid for his six trips to China during the past few years.

Certainly occurrences like the one in Minnesota, and many more where employees were hoodwinked by union organizers, have caused more than 100 newspaper editorials to condemn the EFCA as unwise and unfair. Comments included "The last thing Virginia—or any state—needs now is a monkey wrench the size of card check sticking in the economy's gears (*Richmond Times-Dispatch*, 2/22/09), "Workers deserve to make the choice on union membership through a free and fair process. This bill would ensure neither" (*The Orlando Sentinel*, 2/21/09), "The purposely misnamed 'Employee Free Choice Act' would deny the free choice of secret ballots, and should be rejected" (*Chattanooga Free Press*, 2/08/09), "This legislation would put businesses and workers at a competitive disadvantage," (*The Greenville News*, 2/2/09), and "The 'renaissance' that unions envision to stem three decades of declining membership is a recipe for certain economic disaster" (*Pittsburgh Tribune-Review*, 1/4/09).

To be certain, a strange collection of politicians has opposed the bill including former Senator George McGovern. He called EFCA "a disturbing and undemocratic overreach, not in the interest of either management or labor" while noting, "instead of providing a voice for the unheard, EFCA risks silencing those who would speak." Others who have voiced opposition include Rev. Al Sharpton, former Michigan governor, Presidential candidate Mitt Romney, Nebraska Senator Ben Nelson, and both Democratic Senators from Arkansas.

Leading the charge as the 2009 legislative session began in favor of the bill were Iowa Senator Tom Harkin and Massachusetts Senator Ted Kennedy. Despite their furor to gain passage, Senators such as Lamar Alexander, Republican of Tennessee, voiced opposition with Alexander calling the bill, "The No-Choice Act." Stern certainly must not have liked this depiction, but as he awaited a vote on the legislation, he and the SEIU were hard at work pressuring companies like mine to unionize. Working in the shadows, they had a plan of attack ready, one threatening EMS's future.

Neutrality Agreement–The War Begins

BEGINNING IN LATE 2005, SEIU DIRECTLY TARGETED THREE CITIES in the Midwest: Columbus and Cincinnati, Ohio, and Indianapolis with its Three Cities One Future Campaign. Because EMS had business operations in each, we knew it was only a matter of time until union organizers contacted us.

What I didn't know then, but realized later, were the very simple tactics SEIU implemented—organizers moved into the cities and focused their efforts on the building owners and the companies servicing them. Then they approached the contractors and requested a meeting to discuss unionization.

According to the SEIU business model labeled a "Corporate Campaign," the contractors forced into signing a Neutrality Agreement and negotiating a contract had to represent collectively 60 percent of the commercial cleanable square footage in these cities while the minimum building size was 75,000 to 100,000 square feet. The numbers made unionizing worthwhile for the SEIU from a business perspective. For the three cities mentioned, this meant approximately fifteen hundred janitors/custodians or so could be organized per city—generating close to a half million dollars per city in annual revenues through paid union dues.

Whether it is in one of these cities or another across the country, SEIU basically uses this cookie cutter process whether companies are of high character and strong integrity, or of low character and no integrity. It doesn't matter to them. It is their action plan, and they carry it out the same everywhere they go. Giving credit where it is due, they are quite crafty as to how they roll it out and operate. In Indianapolis, for instance, they targeted businesses in Marion and adjoining Hamilton County and left the rest of the Metropolitan area alone. The idea was to gain a foothold and move on from there. So when organizers said they were fighting for all the janitors in the Indianapolis area, this was really not the case. Instead, SEIU targeted two counties with the most income potential dues-wise, and the heck with the janitors in other counties surrounding Indianapolis. Similarly, in the Cincinnati Metropolitan area, SEIU utilized the same game plan. This is very, very typical of their program, as the union wants people to believe that their motives are altruistic based on sexy slogans such as "raising janitors out of poverty," when the bottom line still is unionizing so revenues from dues increases permitting more money for political agendas.

Having selected the intended targets, the union then set up their infrastructure, one where they selected local organizers willing to work with and represent what I call "front organizations," not-for-profits with inspiring yet mis-leading names such as Jobs with Justice, Interfaith Workers Justice, and United Students to help promote the ensuing campaigns. Before our war with SEIU in Indianapolis, there was not a local Interfaith Workers Justice group, forcing the union to use the Chicago main office to recruit clergy in our area for use in assisting the union with their game plan. Heading this effort would be Rev. Cushman Wood, a member of the Interfaith Workers Justice board. Later, a woman named Allison Luthie would bring Jobs for Justice into the fold as the war escalated. Like those members of United Students, used in Cincinnati, these activist groups, composed of well intended, dedicated-to-their-cause people, were, it appears never provided the true facts causing them to be easily recruited, and easily misled.

Once the organizers and supporting groups are in place, first contact is made with the targeted companies, the cleaners, the business and building owners, and the property managers. With the plan underway, the union organizers meet with the contract-cleaning company owners and ask them to sign a Neutrality Agreement. This document, as noted, is the model for the Employee Free Choice Act from the perspective that 1) the provisions eliminate the secret-ballot election, 2) it requires the employer to provide every employee's name and address, and 3) it prohibits the employer from discussing the union with any of the employees. If it chooses to do so, the union could use the contact information to harass, intimidate, and misinform employees into signing union cards. Once contract-cleaning companies representing 60 percent of the cleanable space in a city sign the Neutrality Agreement and there is a majority of each company's employees who sign union cards, the employers have the obligation to participate in city-wide negotiations with the union.

As part of signing the Neutrality Agreement, the employer agrees not to speak with its employees about the union *regardless of whether the employees ask for information*. Additionally, the company is required to send a letter to all employees indicating the company's neutral stance and that it is in agreement with the union, which for the hourly employees makes it look like the company has caved and they may as well sign the cards. What trickery!

With this plan of attack in mind, the SEIU started its "Corporate Campaign" with GSF (Group Services France), a local company owned by a French conglomerate since the early to mid-1990s. The SEIU picked on GSF who they believed was one of the lower wage-payers in the janitorial ranks operating in Indianapolis. Because it also used what the union believed to be a questionable incentive system that most janitors couldn't achieve, the union saw its opportunity. It put pressure on GSF to sign the Neutrality Agreement, but the company refused. In line with SEIU's preconceived plan, the union then put public relations pressure on Eli Lilly, WellPoint, and the NCAA headquarters, three of GSF's main customers. The threat was obvious: if GSF did not sign a Neutrality Agreement, union members would picket the company's buildings causing a public relations nightmare. Such a threat caused us to lose even the chance to bid for business at companies like Eli Lilly where I was told by an executive that it did not want to take any chance on bad public relations in the form of picketing, etc. This would occur at Wellpoint as well, meaning we lost the potential for millions of dollars in revenues simply because I would not relinquish my employees' rights by signing the Neutrality Agreement. Predictably, as the three companies wanted to avoid added bad press, their executives put pressure on the GSF general manager threatening to cancel their contract. The SEIU even called a so-called "unfair labor practice" strike against GSF, putting added pressure on the cleaning company to sign. Unwilling to permit this to occur, GSF caved in and signed the Neutrality Agreement, the first ones in Indianapolis to do so. I'm sure Stern had a smile on his face when he learned the good news. His plan was working.

To gain a perspective as to how EMS fit into the SEIU plan to organize, some comparisons are worthy. There are several major national cleaning companies, with ABM being the largest one in the world. It is a billion dollar-plus company, and for reasons known only to them, they automatically sign Neutrality Agreements in any city where the SEIU operates. Other large national cleaning companies included One Source, later acquired by ABM, and SBM and a regional company 4M. Each of these companies had acceded to the union's demands. The result: SEIU now had GSF, ABM, SPM, and 4M in tow. Next up on the docket was EMS, as we were one of the largest cleaning companies in the city.

In late December of 2005, SEIU representatives contacted me to arrange a meeting. I finally arranged to have a meeting with Dennis Dingow in April of 2006, the union's contract administrator from Cleveland. He was a mid-50s, medium-built fellow with a friendly attitude, who appeared to be disarming and non-confrontational. Having dealt with this type of person before, it was not difficult to see through a rather thin veneer, one hiding an intense man who I later learned had one goal and one goal only, to intimidate me into signing the Neutrality Agreement.

We enjoyed a fairly friendly meeting at a downtown club. Dennis told me about SEIU and how altruistic they were—interested mainly in improving working hours and working conditions for janitors across the country. When I asked for specifics, and pressed him on it, he could not, or would not, provide any. I explained that for me to consider any union proposal, I would have to better understand what they had in mind.

Dingow agreed to contact me again, but I wasn't holding my breath—Based on some research I had done I knew that facts, ones based on truth, were not part of SEIU's portfolio. Instead, they wanted to work in the margins, with allegations not accusations, all pointing to the end result of having a company cave into their demands. But initially, at least, we wanted to be open-minded as we knew what was coming if continued resistance occurred—pressure just like that imposed on GSF. At the same time Dingow's demand was quite clear: either we sign the Neutrality Agreement or SEIU would embark upon a "Corporate Campaign" against us using one simple argument with little merit, especially in our case: there is strength in numbers, and more means better for janitors represented by the union. When we challenged this assertion by asking "how?" the union leader quickly attempted to divert us to another subject.

When you challenge SEIU organizers about what they have been able to accomplish in other cities, they will change the subject as well since they are very crafty as to how they handle questions asking for facts. But the "or else" message is very clear, as evidenced by a threat I knew about to a fellow business associate by an SEIU organizer to the effect that he better sign the Neutrality Agreement or they would destroy him, ruin him. This sounds to me like Jimmy Hoffa at work using tactics that in my view are unethical, and possibly even illegal.

In their campaign, the SEIU will also point to poor working conditions in the buildings being serviced by contractors like us. But most of the buildings are what are called "Class A" buildings owned by competent developers who care about quality as much as we do. The union's main objection is usually to point to the use of hazardous chemicals, and while some contractors attempt to cut costs by using inferior products, reputable companies like ours would never do such a thing, as the SEIU fully knew. But it didn't matter as before long the term "sweat shop" entered the equation portraying images of dark and dreary southeast Asian plants where workers are treated like animals while being paid fifty cents an hour. The reality is that in my industry the vast majority of the janitors/custodians work in safe environments as most of the plants or buildings cleaned by contractors have less exposure to hazards that we do in our homes. This is where workers work their tails off at an entry-level, but competent wage while performing a very difficult job because it is tough to maintain an acceptable productivity rate while they vacuum, clean, dust, and empty trash cans over a long period of time.

To be certain, the work done by these individuals is vital to the success of any company as poor cleaning procedures leads to a bad health work environment, an environment not conducive to acceptable productivity. Regardless, the union will file complaints with federal agencies to soil the reputations of companies regardless of the lack of merit of the allegations. And the union public relations wing will publicize the allegations so a company's reputation is battered for all its customers and the public at large to see as evidenced by experiences with OSHA and the NLRB. SEIU flyers trumpet allegations such as "EMS is under investigation for multiple labor law violations including . . ." when in reality the investigation was based on the union's own trumped up charges! Soon, we are looked at as the "bad guys" trying to prevent worker's rights, a far cry from the truth but more interesting than the truth in the media's eyes.

Viewed through a wide lens, SEIU goals are easy to pinpoint. Keep throwing spitballs at the targeted companies until something sticks forcing executives to throw in the towel and agree to be organized. And it works as the toll is heavy for those who decide to stand up for what they believe in and say "no." One kind gentleman I know was at the point where he decided simply to sell his business when things turned sour, or just close it, and walk away. Another in Cincinnati who decided to make a stand nearly ended up in a divorce before finally signing the Neutrality Agreement. In the far west, one business owner filed lawsuits against SEIU while spending, as EMS would have to do, thousands of dollars in legal fees while taking way too much time away from his wife and family dealing with such matters. A fellow businessman fought long and hard, and his health suffered as a result.

One common SEIU tactic is to falsely proclaim that an employer pays poverty wages and publicly vilify the employer for doing so. Regardless of our paying some of the highest wages in the industry, and certainly higher than the union contracts in the cities where we do business, we were lumped in with others who did not do so. Hell with the facts, of course, causing us to look like money-grubbing business owners hurting the little guy or gal when nothing was further from the truth. They conveniently forget that companies, not unions, create jobs. But the union didn't care because it had to make these accusations to rally those in the community they needed to assist their cause.

Examples of union infiltration allegedly based on improving employee wages abound. A couple of years ago, the union in Houston touted their ability to gain a six dollar per hour wage despite the fact that in many cases the employees in the city were making more, except possibly for those who were illegal or undocumented. But once again the union didn't care, dues are dues whether the workers are legal or not. And I will bet that some of the undocumented workers were actually making less than six dollars per hour because they were afraid of being reported and deported. With companies like EMS, this is not an issue as we don't hire undocumented workers—never have, never will. Like many other reputable companies, we carry out stringent background checks, I-9 checks using the government's e-verify program, and other document checks to make certain we are hiring properly documented workers.

Regarding wage levels—in cities where EMS operates, our wages and certainly the benefit packages including health care and vacation are far superior to those negotiated by SEIU. Interestingly enough, our company not only provides better wages and benefits, but also permits people who work 30 hours or more to qualify as full-time, earning health care benefits. In contrast, the SEIU Indianapolis and Cincinnati contracts require workers to spend at least 35 hours on the job to be eligible for health care benefits. Normally union health care benefits don't kick in until two to three years after the contract has been negotiated. But SEIU press releases never mention these points because it is not in the union's best interest to do so. Instead, the union boasts about the great package the workers are getting which is nothing more than a smoke screen, plus the employees are now paying dues. What the union never tells anyone concerns the first two items that are non-negotiable for them. Items that will cause the union to make major concessions at the expense of the employees: 1) A union security clause that requires all eligible employees to pay union dues. (In other words, even if you voted against the union you still have to pay dues and initiation fees as a condition of employment.) 2) Check-off clauses forcing the company to collect dues from the employee's paychecks. (They don't trust the employees to keep paying, and the unions keep their administrative costs down.)

Unions like SEIU will also tell support groups, those "front organizations" I mentioned, that we are not paying a "living wage," thus preying on their sympathies for the poor plight of the workers when in fact, none of those in the support groups has taken time to learn that our employees are actually treated well. Why? Because this union doesn't give a damn, but instead wants to destroy the reputation of a company like EMS so we will sign the Neutrality Agreement leading to provisions like the ones featured in the Employee Free Choice Act.

To present some numbers (please note that I wasn't much of a math student in college), let's say you have 20 part-time people working in a building for four hours a night—eighty man/woman hours in all. During contract negotiations, the union over the course of the agreement secures full-time employment, then instead of 20 people at four hours a night, the number is reduced to ten people working eight hours a night. So while requiring more employees to work full time jobs (and thereby qualify for high priced union health care benefits), the union has effectively eliminated half of the jobs in the building. This in turn, though the union doesn't want to mention it, causes the unemployment rolls to increase. Also, if the people get paid more, the hours will be reduced. Why? Because building owners and managers cannot pay more, the contractor will reduce the total hours worked every night. Fewer workers are needed and although those left may be taking home more money, they are working twice as hard, something the union professes to want to eliminate but actually encourages through its programs.

Unions like the SEIU also point to employees needing to be unionized because employers supposedly intimidate, harass, and abuse them, and they have nowhere to go with their complaints without union representation. But in today's marketplace, very rarely does this occur, especially at companies like EMS where employees are valued, not chastised. But the union would like people to believe that we are back in the 1930s and 1940s when we had sweatshops, kids were employed, people were working 80 hours a week, and there was no overtime pay or benefits. Today, we have federal and state laws and government regulatory agencies (EEOC, OSHA, DOL) protecting these safeguards. And the country has become more civilized; employers understand that people have to have free time and the ability to do other things. Regardless, unions are stuck in time and are becoming extinct like the dinosaurs as they will not budge from archaic arguments making little sense in today's modern business world. But when you have no real arguments to offer on behalf of unionization, old ones must be used as new ones don't make sense. Thus, the unions prey on supporters who simply don't understand the true facts and unfortunately, bless them, get swooped into a crusade where organizing a union is the ultimate answer to a problem that doesn't really exist.

Also, remember, any employee who feels wronged may contact the NLRB and file a complaint, report incidents of abuse to the local law enforcement agency, or file charges with the EEOC or Department of Labor. Chief among Stern's belief that unions must be imposed on every company within an industry is their stand that union companies cannot compete in the marketplace with non-union companies. This simply isn't true. At a university, for instance, where EMS was ingrained as the cleaning provider, a union contractor underbid us when new contracts were being considered. But EMS won the business. Why? Because first, the union contractor could not agree to a three-year contract as required by the university. Second, university officials discovered the union contractor had miscalculated the wage rates they were going to pay. And third, they had no history with the university, causing officials to be skeptical of the union contractor's ability to clean the buildings in a quality manner as we had done for years. So cost is not always the deciding factor with government contracts.

When SEIU learned that the college was standing firm by awarding the business to EMS, they asked for an investigation by the State Attorney General's office. We discovered that the fight might be fixed as several of the state attorneys were former SEIU attorneys. But the university President stuck to his position and resisted any pressure to change his decision. What a strong advocate he was.

An instance where the low bid was the deciding factor in awarding a contract occurred at Sallie Mae in Indianapolis. The competition was between the giant of our industry, ABM, a union contractor, and EMS the incumbent. ABM won with their lower bid as did GSF at the Children's Museum, another account where EMS was the incumbent.

Bidding at the heavyweight developer Duke was between EMS, QBM, ABM, and One Source—the latter two union companies. One Source and ABM were the low bidders and won the majority of the contract, proving once again that union companies may compete with non-union companies such as ours. This points out that decisions are not always based on value. With the Sallie Mae and Duke contracts, cost was the driving factor. These examples clearly show: 1) union companies may compete with regard to cost, 2) SEIU doesn't really care about the employees as in these situations the contractors sacrificed employee wages and hours to be worked in order to secure the business, and 3) the union will still support contractors who have signed the recognition agreement regardless of whether they have good wages and benefits. The reason—an easy and simple one—the union now has more union dues flowing in to fill their coffers. Not much of a pro-employee stance, if you ask me. Even more astounding is that the SEIU and Interfaith Clergy group released statements to customers and the news media praising Duke and Sallie Mae for being responsible corporate citizens by supporting janitors' rights and choosing responsible (i.e. Union) contractors. In fact, the chosen contractors in most cases were actually paying their employees significantly lower wages and providing reduced hours compared to the supposed irresponsible contractors they replaced!

Stern, Dingow, and other SEIU officials would have those criticizing EMS for its non-union stance think otherwise. And this was one of the chief bones of contention when I first met with Dennis, a fellow I enjoyed and respected and would continue to like and respect over the course of our dealings. After our first meeting, I sent him an e-mail telling him it was great to meet a good old Catholic boy from Cleveland like him, because in the spirit of cooperation, I wanted to maintain a good relationship and see if there was anything to be gained by EMS's involvement with the SEIU. Later, the e-mail system caused hard feelings when, prior to discovering a problem on his end, Dennis became upset, thinking I hadn't returned his e-mail messages to him. To clear things up, we held a second meeting where I brought along my legal counsel, and he invited his boss, Peter Hanrahan, SEIU's Region 3 President. As the aroma of good food swept through the dining room, we chatted about health care cost and other matters, but I soon realized Dennis had the impression I was going to sign the Neutrality Agreement. I wasn't, however, and I made my intention quite clear. He returned to Cleveland very displeased, and instead of corresponding with me, he sent e-mails to our attorney. In September 2006, Dennis's frustration peaked and he sent a scathing e-mail. Accusations abounded with the bottom line being,

• • • • • • • • • •

If Dave Bego expects special treatment he is about to have a very rude awakening. If your [legal counsel's] advice to your client is that they can weather the storm so to speak, then so be it. Mr. Bego has had at least three months to make his considerations. We will give him thirty more days. I do not find it amusing to see a smile on his face every time we speak of some other contractor we have engaged in our targeting when his accounts remain incident free. I believe in conversation over confrontation [but] the conversation must produce results though; when it doesn't then it may require confrontation. If Mr. Bego believes that his salesmanship is so much better than everyone else, he has much more to gain than to lose. That is his choice now.

• • • • • • • • • • • • • •

Basically, Dennis was giving me 30 days to sign the Neutrality Agreement, or else. This was confirmed by another e-mail in early October where he wrote: "Where are we? We need an answer, not more time. Both Pittsburgh and St. Louis are waiting to hear from me. Both are prepared to run campaigns as we are in Indianapolis. We ask for a relationship, and if you want that then let's move this forward. Regards, Dennis." My response was short and to the point: "Dennis, I appreciate all the time and hard work you have dedicated to supplying information requested by EMS. After review of the information provided, EMS does not feel it is in the best interests of its employees to pursue this relationship at this time. Best Regards."

Despite being at loggerheads with Dennis, pre-war negotiations with him had provided insight into what their next steps would be. But when I walked around our offices, or at home in the yard where I could think clearly, I kept returning to something Dennis said when we first met. As I said, we had enjoyed a fairly amicable lunch up to the time where Dennis started pressing me again about signing the Neutrality Agreement and I indicated that was not going to occur. His face turned a bit red as he looked away, and then he said six words that triggered the start of a three-year war —"We like conversation, but embrace confrontation," almost the exact phrase Stern had used in his book, one that Dennis had obviously read.

Realizing that the SEIU would take action against EMS, our employees, and our customers, I had to restrain myself from making a scene. Instead, the goodbyes were short and curt, with Dennis still somehow believing I would change my mind. As he and Stern soon discovered, I wasn't about to.

The Assault

ALL THE WHILE, STRONG INDICATIONS THE WAR WAS ABOUT TO BEGIN had occurred with split-second precision.

The SEIU union soldiers were ready to pounce on EMS and I knew it based on an August 21, 2006 incident at Market Tower, one of our downtown Indianapolis clients. Here the first of hundreds of "incident reports" would be chronicled, ones filling two large-notebooks by the time spring 2009 approached. If I were going to war with SEIU, then we were going to keep accurate records every step of the way. If we couldn't outmaneuver the enemy due to their unlimited financial resources and political clout, perhaps we could "out-organize" them as I had the sneaking feeling Mr. Stern and his SEIU colleagues had never faced a tenacious opponent, one that was going to fight them for as long as it took to destroy their willingness to fight causing them to leave us alone. This way, our employees' rights to freedom would be protected; my one and only goal in taking on the monster SEIU.

As reported by one of our building managers, an employee named Roberto was walking into the Market Tower building when a union organizer approached him. He gave Roberto a card and began asking questions about wages and the hours he worked. When Roberto provided no information, the organizer asked for his card back stating, "I don't want anyone to find out that the union was around." As he left, he told Roberto he could visit his house if he wanted to know more about the union, but Roberto told him he was "happy working for EMS." Three days later, the same organizer appeared and confronted a fellow named Luis near his car parking space. Luis brushed him off, but the organizer hung around for a while before leaving.

Such incidents made me certain it was time to create a battle plan to combat the ensuing SEIU tactics. Doing so was completely against everything I stood for, as I had created EMS to be a "below the radar" company with little fanfare in the public eye. We never asked for publicity nor relished it. Instead, we were what I would call a "quiet" company that simply went about its job with efficiency and enjoyed staying out of the newspaper headlines. Modesty and humility are two characteristics I applaud in people and we sought to run EMS with those qualities in mind. Above all, as I always told my management colleagues and employees alike, we were in a "relationship business," and this meant securing solid relationships with all of our customers. We wanted to be honest, professional, and take care of customers with a sense of urgency.

But, with SEIU lurking at the gate, I realized a plan was necessary. With this in mind, I knew we had to prepare our employees and our customers for what might lie ahead as the war escalated. Once we completed this task, we could organize the forces at our disposal, management colleagues who had worked with me over the years when any sort of crisis occurred. We would add to them a crack, specialized legal team familiar with labor issues. Then with our army in ready-mode, would fend off the enemy at every turn even if it meant media exposure and several rounds of battle at the NLRB trying to convince them EMS was the good guy and the SEIU was the bad guy.

This was necessary as EMS customers in Indianapolis, Cincinnati, Ft. Myers and Jacksonville, Wichita, and Tucson, would soon be receiving anti-EMS letters condemning us on every front. For a time, we could not figure out how SEIU had obtained a list of our customers to the extent of wondering if we had a "mole" in our midst supplying the information. But finally we discovered the truth—SEIU had secured a copy of our company newsletter, one published for the benefit of employees. Complimentary customer letters were featured, and the union had used those names to send their mailings.

Every day when I awoke, I was ready for another boxing match. Sleep didn't come as easy as before, as I watched with interest for SEIU's next moves. On January 3, 2007, after the holiday break, the SEIU's Local 3 representative Rebecca Maran left her business card at the Sallie Mae building in Indianapolis. Then flyers were handed out at the end of the month proclaiming, "EMS, the janitorial company contracted at Market Tower, has threatened and tried to intimidate janitors who have stood up for better working conditions." Specific allegations included: "Threatening and intimidating janitors to coerce them from exercising their rights," "Interrogating janitors in violation of their protected rights," and "Retaliating against janitors for participating in protected activity."

On February 9, four to six union protesters appeared on the sidewalk in front of the building. Later on, we discovered that when SEIU could not round up enough EMS employees to picket, they created an interesting, if downright deceiving, alternative. We knew because one of our facility managers, unable to recognize a man on the picket line, asked him "Are you are a member of the union?" He replied, "No, I'm from the Wheeler Mission [an urban homeless shelter] and they paid me to come down here and picket for the day." Because apparently the man was paid in cash, there was no record of his being used as a dupe while all the while causing those watching the demonstration to believe EMS employees or union organizers were backing the campaign. Four days later, the campaign intensified. An SEIU organizer violated EMS's employee Fred's right to privacy by visiting his home where the organizer attempted to convince him to sign a union authorization card. Fred refused, but this didn't alter my feelings of anger over him being disturbed at home. Fred was a good employee and he didn't deserve to be treated in such a shabby way.

On April 6, I wrote to our "valued customers" expressing my knowledge that they had "received written propaganda being circulated in various forms by the SEIU." I told them, "Because of the widespread and malicious nature of this propaganda, I wanted to take the time to respond to these false accusations and tell the truth about the SEIU and the company's response to these actions." After explaining that the union had launched a "campaign of harassment against EMS" in order to "smear the company's reputation in an attempt to try to convince our customers to stop doing business with EMS," the letter informed customers that SEIU's intent was to "pressure us into signing their Neutrality Agreement," which, in turn, would relinquish my employees' rights to a secret-ballot election. This, I explained, would force me to remain silent on union issues and require that I provide confidential information about the employees. Information I knew would be used to pressure my employees into signing union cards against their will.

Because I wanted the customers to know the truth, we listed 10 bullet-point factors affecting the SEIU attack. Among them were the fact that we valued the employees, and provided "excellent employee training to our management staff" so as to "treat all employees fairly regardless of whether they support unionization or not." We pointed out the competitive wage and benefit page as well and added, "EMS provides high-quality equipment and chemicals through our own high-quality supply company while placing continued emphasis on employee safety." Mentioned also was our assurance that despite the SEIU claims to the contrary, EMS employees have never been asked to handle human body parts and will never handle them in the future, a reference to the university fiasco. I told customers "there is absolutely no merit to any of the union's allegations against the company," before closing with, "It is unfortunate that the SEIU has decided to engage in this malicious campaign against EMS, and we regret any inconvenience you may have been caused."

To bolster our cause, we then sent a copy of an article by national radio talk show host Lowell Ponte about Stern and the SEIU. A portion read:

• • • • • • • • • •

SEIU and its political, media, and leftwing activist allies conspire to attack a company directly with what they call "Corporate Campaign" or the "death of a thousand cuts." Like the Furies of Greek mythology, this cabal of attackers harasses and disrupts company activities, sends vicious e-mails and letters to stockholders, intimidates customers, stalks and frightens employees, files baseless lawsuits, plants false stories with media allies to smear the company's reputation, and uses hundreds of other tactics to injure the targeted company in every way they can imagine . . . The aim of this concerted swarming attack is to bully and pressure a targeted company into signing an agreement making SEIU the representative of its employees.

• • • • • • • • • • • • • •

To my way of thinking, Ponte nailed it listing the exact tactics being used against my beloved company. Hopefully his strong words and my explanations made our customers as upset as it did me as the "cabal of attackers" kept up the pressure day after day.

To further inform customers as to the lies being told about EMS, we sent them a page called "EMS: Janitors for Truth." Discrepancies galore were displayed indicating the false SEIU claims.

Regarding my need to alert field employees to the anticipated attacks, a speech I gave at the university was symbolic of the information I wanted to disseminate. I first gave the audience a bit of my background informing them I was anything but anti-union based on previous experience at union companies and plants. I told them about EMS and how we started with nothing, not one customer, and had grown over the years, thanks in large part to their hard work. Turning to the SEIU, the explanation was given that it might be perceived as a union, but in fact it was a business with its main goal to collect union dues. And the only way to collect more dues was to organize more workers by telling lies about companies like mine that treated employees with respect and paid fair wages with fair benefits. Believing they should understand why the SEIU had targeted our company, I presented the facts involved before emphatically stating, so there would be no question of my intent: "I can tell you our stance will continue to be that we are not going to allow this pressure to change our mind. We are not going to sign a Neutrality Agreement that eliminates employees' right to a secret-ballot election."

Then I hit them with some numbers. I explained that, for instance, inside the St. Louis beltway, a union contract included a top starting rate of about 6 dollars and 75 cents per hour. Outside the beltway it was about 7 dollars and 25 cents per hour. Because Cincinnati was about the same size as St. Louis, we expected the rates to be similar. With these numbers rolling around in their heads, I then told them what they already knew—that they were making more than that with the chance to better it based on job performance and time spent employed by the company. "What happens then," I asked, "if the union negotiates a rate of 7 dollars and 25 cents per hour for everyone? Do those making more have to make less again?" The answer, "Yes, this could occur."

As I watched the employees, it was easy to tell what I was saying was contrary to what union organizers had told them. Continuing, I made it clear that EMS was committed to doing the best we could for our employees anytime we bid on a job by trying to attain the best wages possible. I said that sometimes we were more successful than others, but that we tried to show the customer it was in their best interest to pay the employees more from a productivity, quality, and longevity standpoint by being fair.

Realizing the workers had heard of sky-high 12 to 15 dollar-per-hour promises, I told them I doubted this was possible. Maybe such wages could be paid in larger cities, but not in Cincinnati. One of our employees, quick to understand the intent of my words, cut me off and commented that such pie-in-the-sky wages might occur in Chicago or Pittsburgh, but not in Cincinnati where the cost of living was lower.

Having given them the financial lowdown, I turned to the Neutrality Agreement and what signing it meant for EMS. I told them why we would not sign it, and to watch out for guarantees SEIU made to them because they couldn't follow through because their whole platform was a house of cards. Questions from the workers focused on such topics as wage differentials between different cleaning companies, the employee handbook section outlawing MP players and I-Pods (dangerous for the workers in case of emergency), union contact was their right, and no interference would come from EMS—matters like that. I closed with a "Thank you," hoping I had at least driven home our side of the argument.

Meanwhile, my daughter Kelly met with employees[1] at the Sallie Mae building in Indianapolis. She let them know the lowdown—that demonstrations may occur. Kelly said the employees were certainly free to talk to union organizers, but that the SEIU's intent was to persuade workers to sign cards so the union could represent them. She cautioned them to not believe all the promises the union made. As she spoke, new employee handbooks were passed out and each employee was required to sign a receipt of acceptance for record keeping purposes. These handbooks explained our rules and standards of conduct. Kelly then reviewed EMS's union-free policy, also explained in the handbook, before

---

[1]To protect the identity of EMS employees and others, alternative names have been used in this book.

asking if there were any questions. When there were none, the meeting was over. She was pleased with the exchange of information and felt confident the workers were as well.

Despite Kelly's and EMS's good intentions, less than a month later, SEIU filed charges against her alleging threatening remarks and intimidation. Two employees, one who had a poor attendance record and eventually had to be dismissed, and the other, a fellow who threatened both an EMS supervisor and manager with bodily harm in front of a security guard and was dismissed, led the charge. Having my daughter as the target of such an attack caused me to cringe and made me wonder whether the fight was worth it. Kelly a competitor in the mold of her dad looked forward to the day when she could defend her reputation in front of the NLRB. Thankfully, she was ultimately vindicated when an Administrative Law Judge of the NLRB found no merit to these allegations.

The conflict with SEIU at Sallie Mae was particularly disturbing as workers were earning a higher wage even on the third shift. This was unusual. In many SEIU contracts shift differentials do not exist as the union simply lumps together all hourly workers and classification wages. This propagates sameness and suppresses individualism and self-determination, a major union goal. Why? Because keeping everyone equal reduces friction—important as the union does not have to spend time resolving differences.

Regardless, the two young people who were influenced by the SEIU to file affidavits charging violations in the meeting against Kelly had been prompted during a dinner after work where union organizers displayed their impressive buttons and exaggerated what was going to occur if the workers joined. I'm sure the one fellow who had attendance problems listened and swallowed the union horse phooey with full effect. His attacking us was particularly disturbing as he didn't have a car to drive to work and an EMS supervisor picked him up out of the kindness of his heart. Many times he was late for the pickup, but none of this information surfaced when the SEIU grandstanded by filing the charges. All they cared about was making us look bad even though we had strong procedures in place regarding the firing of anyone; human resources had conducted a full investigation before this occurred. The reason? From the day I created EMS, I was determined that every employee regardless of age, race, religion, national origin, disability or other characteristics, would always be given a fair chance and due process. Procedures were put in place early for a fair discipline procedure. More importantly, we took away the final decision to fire an employee from the managers in the field. We did this to protect workers from bad or unfair managers, incomplete investigations, personality differences, or other extreme circumstances. I believe these procedures along with a commitment to hire and train good managers is the reason why over the years we have had very few EEOC (Equal Employment Opportunity Commission) complaints and have always been vindicated in those claims.

When Kelly was charged, this was certainly one of the darkest days of the war. I had spent years building a business, a reputable one, and in the process, creating jobs for employees who really wanted to get ahead. And so many of them did, that I felt good at the end of the day; I was truly helping people. No, I couldn't pay these hardworking people sky-high wages, but I could pay them as much as possible according to industry standards while still permitting EMS to be competitive. Ninety-nine percent of the employees realized this but two disgruntled ones caused us to defend ourselves. All the while I never received any correspondence, telephone call, or any other communication from an employee asking me to recognize the union or telling me that they wanted to organize. And why should they when deep in their heart each knew EMS treated them better than any other company in our industry—bar none.

Regardless, having explained as best we could to customers and employees alike our position, I could only hope our plan would succeed. If we could knock SEIU out of the box, then EMS and its employees could declare a victory, one for the little guy fighting the big union boss and his vast number of union organizers. Only time would tell who would win the war, but I was confident that EMS could hold its own with Stern and the SEIU, if we stayed on course and never backed down.

To their credit, the union kept up the relentless attacks. At one point, organizers attempted to embarrass me during a golf tournament at a local course. Several appeared with signs stating "Shame on EMS" while chanting "EMS Must Go, Dave Bego Must Go." If Stern had been with them, he would have become target practice for some very unhappy golfers including me. Hopefully all of those disturbing the day were truly union workers, not shills as was the case in downtown Indianapolis. I did not recognize any EMS employees; this was reassuring. On the drive home from the course, I was thankful for the support from the course members, but upset over being verbally assaulted in front of my friends.

Meanwhile, SEIU organizers appeared at a large EMS pharmaceutical customer of ours and attempted to speak to employees as they arrived for work or as they left at the end of their shift. They were escorted off the grounds by the company's security. Next, the organizers chose Indianapolis Power and Light's corporate headquarters on the circle in the downtown area to distribute handbills. Simultaneously, protesters distributing flyers stood outside Market Tower, the building later shown on a Lou Dobbs CNN special about Stern, the SEIU, and our company. None of those protesting or distributing handbills were EMS employees. One of the handbills included the language, "EMS keeps janitors in Poverty and has sought to prevent them from exercising their rights." EMS employee Daniel was quoted as saying,

"Working at EMS I feel like I am being used for my hard work rather than appreciated . . . I do not have health benefits working with EMS . . . the wages are not enough to support a single person, let alone a man with a wife and six children . . . ." Little did those who saw the flyers realize that Daniel, like so many other unsuspecting workers, was being used by the SEIU. How I wished I could get a bullhorn and scream the truth so our side of the story could be heard.

No one listening or watching the demonstration knew that Daniel had an extremely poor attendance and performance track record and was eventually terminated for theft, factors undoubtedly influencing his comments. We also eventually learned he had been hired as an SEIU organizer. I suspect poor Daniel's performance problems and eventual termination were all pre-meditated, staged acts encouraged by the union so they could file unfair labor practices against EMS and use them to defame the company in flyers and letters. This also positioned them for a last desperate act to force me to sign a Neutrality Agreement.

Meanwhile, the war continued. On March 13, as spring began to peek out with warmer temperatures, SEIU organizers solicited EMS employees in front of a customer's building in

Cincinnati before their shift telling them the union could get them "12 to 15 dollars per hour," a totally bogus guarantee. A day later, approximately 8 to 10 organizers protested. To make a media splash, several organizers appeared five days later and demonstrated using a jail cell type prop. Inside the cardboard box painted to look like a jail cell, they had positioned a person wearing an EMS shirt. Emblazoned on the front were the words, "EMS Poverty Prison." One handbill read, "Janitors Sentenced to Life in Working Poverty by EMS Janitorial."

Hearing of these incidents and reading the handbills and flyers was difficult because I knew they were based on untruths. I kept trying to be calm, but when my blood pressure rose to the level where I wanted to march down to a building and shout out the truth for all to hear, prayer comforted me. Seeing workers used for union purposes hurt the most as I knew these workers did not realize they were being used. They were simply pawns in a chess game Stern and the SEIU were playing in the hope that I would cave into their demands. Tears came to my eyes when I thought of how hard I had worked, how hard all of us at EMS had worked to build a quality company with an unblemished track record of caring for our employees. Now mud was being slung at us from every corner, and all I could do was hope my customers would remain loyal and not dump us, and that friends and colleagues who knew me would stand by our side based on knowledge that EMS was the victim of unwarranted character assassination. But Stern and his union organizers didn't care what I thought; they didn't care at all about any of that.

This was proven when the union filed charges against our company with the NLRB. They included allegations at Sallie Mae for forced removal of union buttons, interrogation, impression of surveillance, and for threatening employees with job loss. In quick succession, SEIU told our customers we were "under investigation," terminology designed to scare the customers into canceling contracts with us. If they did so, and others followed, there would be the choice as to whether to sign the piece of paper agreeing to be bound by the Neutrality Agreement, or face possible loss of the business if things progressed to that point because of loss of necessary revenues. EMS was also leaking money through retention of attorneys providing expert advice as to how to deal with Stern and SEIU. How I hated to approve hefty checks for attorney fees and other costs needed to fight the union. But I refused to give up everything I believed in and let my company and my employees down. This would never have been necessary if Stern's appointed organizer Dennis Dingow had provided me with proof that the SEIU could truly be a partner in helping my employees instead of starting a war to destroy the company or force union recognition on my employees through manipulation and intimidation. At least nearly all of the EMS employees understood the threat and proved it by not signing union cards.

To take advantage of the NLRB filings and their potential impact, about a dozen protesters gathered on two occasions outside a customer's building in Cincinnati. They blocked the sidewalks while carrying flyers with new inflammatory language: "Charges at the National Labor Relations Board include allegations of EMS Management: Threatening and Intimidating janitors to coerce them from exercising their rights, Interrogating janitors in violation of their protected rights, Retaliating against janitors for participating in protected activity." When I saw this flyer, I had to take my hat off to the SEIU strategists as without a whiff of proof regarding any of the allegations, just posting them made us look guilty despite the fact the allegations were completely baseless, containing not a shred of truth. This was in line with the union's smart idea to "allege" but never "accuse." How I wanted to reciprocate, but this is what they wanted from me—reactions further blemishing our company's image. I was not about to give them that satisfaction or stoop to their level. I was determined to remain professional.

On March 22, the protesters appeared and were removed by security guards at the pharmaceutical company again. The intensity of the protests continued with organized demonstrations at IPL, Sallie Mae, and in Cincinnati.

When I believed the war could not become more bizarre, it did. Without warning, SEIU filed an OSHA complaint in Cincinnati against EMS. This government agency, the Occupational Safety and Health Administration, establishes and enforces protective standards designed to prevent work-related injury illnesses and death. The complaint charged that EMS employees were carrying human body parts out in bags at the university; that there were hazardous chemicals and dust in the bio lab, and that people were getting nose bleeds from the poor conditions. Then the SEIU sent out handbills and letters alleging that EMS was being investigated for OSHA violations at the university. Using the word "investigated" had its obvious repercussions, a crafty move by the union. Of course, when the truth was revealed, it became known that the lab in question was a regular biology lab anyone in college might experience. There was no dust found, no hazardous materials of any kind, animal parts from dissections existed, but no EMS employees touched or disposed of them.

The university's own investigation confirmed these facts, and their independent report was forwarded to OSHA. It promptly dismissed the charges. Regardless, SEIU had used a completely innocuous situation and filed trumped-up charges against EMS in order to defame our company and the university. When I thought of what had occurred, I wondered whether people like Stern and his band of thugs had any sense of shame. Apparently they did not, and realizing this, we decided to confront any and all of the accusations against EMS by suggesting a meeting between Cincinnati's Mayor, Deputy Mayor, the Cincinnati City Council, customers and everyone concerned including the SEIU, and me. But being held accountable at a public forum was not something the union was interested in and they canceled the meeting. Working in the shadows was one thing, but having to defend their positions in the light of day in front of God and everyone was quite another.

Such a meeting was necessary, I felt, as the customer was in the midst of attempting to construct a new building, a project requiring Cincinnati city council approval. The deputy mayor and some members of the city council had been besieged with union propaganda about how EMS was low on the wage, benefit, and hours worked front. We were also accused of underbidding union companies because of our non-union status. Regarding this latter charge, the SEIU would have been crucified as I was prepared to relate the details of the cleaning contract just awarded at Cincinnati International Airport. The incumbent, ABM, was evidently failing because it paid such low wages that it could not keep workers on the job despite a nearly 1,000,000 dollar-a-year contract. When bidding opened for a new agreement, EMS was asked to bid, and we did, but ended up in the middle of the pack behind three union contractors including a regional contractor, the eventual winner. Our bid was rejected because we factored in higher per hour wages for workers in the range of nine-plus dollars compared with the winning contractor using the proposed union scale range of seven dollars to seven dollars and 50 cents per hour. This was the amount the union would end up negotiating with contractors who signed the bargaining agreement with the SEIU in Cincinnati.

The winning contractor's proposal was almost sixty thousand dollars a year less than the incumbent, and 250,000 dollars less than EMS's bid. The hours required to complete the job were mandatory and because this was a public bid, all the figures were available to the public. When they were exposed, it was clear that the SEIU was not at all interested in doing the right thing for the employees but instead committed to an employer that paid lower wages only because that employer was a so called "responsible contractor," meaning a union contractor. When the SEIU realized we were going to destroy their untrue claims in a face-face confrontation, union officials decided to cancel the meeting. Allegations were one thing—proof quite another.

At the end of the month, about 30 people protested at a Cincinnati customer's building, making loud noises, banging on drums and things of that nature. Handbills were distributed stating, "EMS: The Cleaning Company with DIRTY Secrets."

Losing bids to union companies was commonplace, not the exception, as the SEIU portrayed it. A perfect example occurred when a prominent Indianapolis Developer asked us to bid. They were a huge developer with more than three and a half million square feet of space in the Indianapolis area. I told the executive that EMS didn't stand a chance as companies like ABM would submit much lower bids based on lower worker wages and reduced hours. But he wanted us to bid, and so we did, but our bid was about a third higher than the winners, ABM, One Source, and another local company, a tenant.

When the executive called me with the expected bad news telling me "reputable companies" had prevailed, I asked him if this meant that they would not steal from them. Before he could answer, I also asked the question as to whether these companies could provide the type of detail, hours and wage rates, to support their claims of performing the specifications in the request for pricing. He assured me all was well, and we were left to see what might develop. Unfortunately, it seems they made a decision based not just on price, but on the fact the SEIU had threatened them with bad publicity. I empathize with their plight.

Almost a year and a half later, one of our managers was asked by one of their tenants to clean a building temporarily until some significant problems (worker theft and illegal aliens on the crew) were resolved.

While our manager and her crew were cleaning the facility, several important facts were discovered. First the building condition from a cleaning perspective was sub-par. Second, time sheets revealed that upon calculation, the building was being cleaned almost a third faster than normal for that type of facility. It was now easy to understand why EMS was outbid by almost 30 percent as the winning bidder had reduced the hours spent to clean the building by the same amount. Also, the wages were at the union negotiated level of seven dollars to seven dollars and 50 cents per hour compared with EMS's 1 dollar more per hour.

On March 30, the union rolled out another disturbing tactic designed to make me sign the Neutrality Agreement. Officials sent a letter to several of our customers alluding to the NLRB and OSHA charges. A portion read, "EMS is facing increasing scrutiny for charges it engaged in unlawful labor practices and violated federal law. The charges are part of a growing case against EMS that raises questions about the impact of the cleaning company's business and labor practices on workers and the community." The charges referred to were, of course, the very ones the SEIU themselves, not our employees had filed, not out of conviction for the truth, but for the sole purpose of pressuring EMS into submission.

In the end, these charges against us would amount to nothing with dismissals all around or settlements where we admitted no wrongdoing in the interest of moving on. But this did not stop the SEIU bandwagon from marching forward. At the beginning of April, three men boldly attempted to walk into the university President's office saying they had issues with the health and safety of janitorial workers. The President's secretary and another employee stopped them, and they were escorted away. To his credit, the President never bowed to union tactics. He was loyal to our cause as so many others would be. Thank God for them since they recognized the truth and decided to do the right thing.

Harassment on All Fronts

ON APRIL 6, AS EMS EMPLOYEE PEARL STEPPED OFF A BUS ON HER WAY to work at a building in downtown Cincinnati, two SEIU operatives fell in beside her. Startled by their presence and how close they were to her, she tried to get away from them. Despite asking the two men to leave her alone, they continued alongside, talking at a fast pace about the union. When they arrived at the building door, they stopped her, looked at her face, and one said, "EMS is going to be a part of the union, no matter what, and the union will remember who helps them."

This obvious threat disturbed Pearl and was typical of the lengths to which SEIU would go to get their way. If EFCA is passed, imagine how much pressure, intimidation, and threatening behavior will occur if employees lose their right to private, secret-ballot elections. Senator Arlen Spector, the Pennsylvania Republican turned Democrat, appears to be one who understands how this type of intimidation will occur if the card check process becomes the law of the land. Hopefully his switching parties will not change his position on this issue as he is right, dead right.

When I think of this poor woman, a woman who just wanted to be left alone so she could do her job, it makes me wonder about the ethics of the SEIU. And how so many who are pro-union simply do not know the truth about how these organizers work—how they don't give a damn while trying to impose their will on someone like Pearl a good worker who was scared for her life. But some people just don't get it, especially those with good intentions but confused ideals, agendas, and attitudes.

One such group is the Interfaith Workers Justice (IWJ) Group. On April 10, 2007, SEIU began another phase of its campaign to break us by using this organization to pressure the pharmaceutical executives into demanding that I sign the Neutrality Agreement. This added a new, unexpected element to the equation as clergy influence was now another weapon SEIU would use to make me cave in to their demands.

When I inspected the letter, I noticed the names of two clergy at the top: Rev. Darren Cushman-Wood, and Rev. C. J. Hawking, members of the Indianapolis Clergy Committee. The address was somewhere in Chicago, and I wondered why an organization that far away would be interested in labor issues in Indianapolis. Little did I know that this organization was a strong ally of SEIU and would do all it could to organize as many businesses like mine as possible. In fact, the Interfaith Workers Justice Group headquartered in Chicago according to unionfacts.com received one hundred thousand dollars in support from the SEIU in both 2005 and 2006.

The letter's first line read, "As ambassadors for over 125 clergy in Indianapolis, we arrive at your office today to express a deep concern about the contracting companies you have hired for janitorial services." The text then specified that the organization believed that "all workers need to be paid a living wage, offered affordable family health care, and given a permanent voice on the job." Having stated their purpose, the IWJ alleged, "EMS does not provide a living wage to janitors. This forces many janitors to work two or

three jobs, rendering them absent from their families . . . ."
Attached were the names of the selected clergy who
allegedly supported the words IWJ employed in the letter.
They included Rev. Wood, the author of a book titled *Blue
Collar Jesus*. He was a man with whom I would wrestle for
the duration of the war while attempting to open his eyes as
to the snake-oil character of Stern and the SEIU.

According to his biography book jacket cover, Rev. Wood
graduated from the University of Evansville before studying
at Union Theological Seminary in New York City. Later,
he became the senior minister at Speedway [IN] United
Methodist Church but a passion for labor issues triggered an
adjunct professorship in labor studies at Indiana University.
According to one of the endorsers for his book, Rev. Wood,
a board member of the National Interfaith Committee for
Worker Justice, believed "Christianity is for human rights
for workers," a bold statement, but a worthy one. Somehow
this type of belief had led him to support SEIU and its
organizing agenda.

In his book, Rev. Wood, a mid-50s, medium height,
paunchy fellow sporting a bald head, glasses and graying
beard made it clear that he wholeheartedly supported the
union movement in its entirety, based on religious principles:
"Catholic social teaching has consistently affirmed the
rights of working people to the basic human needs for just
compensation, dignity, and the right to organize labor unions.
Indeed, unions are seen as a legitimate way to express human
solidarity and to contribute to the common good. They are
an effective instrument of economic justice." Reading this
generalization made me question whether I agreed with
his assumption, especially his belief that "Catholic social
teaching" endorsed "the right to organize labor unions."
This seemed a bit of a stretch but if the union was truly
attempting to protect workers as an "effective instrument
of economic justice," I was all for it. But was this the aim of
Stern and the SEIU? From what I had seen thus far, it did
not appear to be so.

Rev. Wood later expressed his belief that "for over 100 years, American Catholics have responded to church teachings with active support for organized labor" before adding a caveat I agreed with, "At times, this support has been tempered by sharp opposition to socialistic and communistic elements within the labor movement." While I was certain Stern was not a communist, despite a fellow union leader's comparisons of him to Vladimir Putin in the newspaper, Stern's socialistic tendencies made me wonder whether clergy like Rev. Wood might disagree with Stern's agenda if he knew and understood the truth behind SEIU.

One thing was for certain, Rev. Wood's beliefs were strong when it came to comparisons between good, old-fashioned capitalism and mankind's inclination toward sinful conduct. Expressing his view regarding connections with the image of God, he wrote, "Sin, then is anything created by human beings—any attitude, action, program, policy, custom, or system—that distorts and diminishes the image of God." By that definition, *capitalism, as it is currently structured,* is sinful. The reason: "It alienates and suppresses the creativity of human work." Such a statement made me shake my head and wonder how this suppression might stifle employees interested in working hard and earning a living wage because at EMS they were free from union restrictions and could vote their conscience in an election without fear of repercussion. I also wondered whether being an advocate of capitalism made me a sinner in God's image. How could that be if my first priority at EMS was protecting the employees and trying to make their life better with a steady job, good wages, and benefits unmatched in my industry? I also wondered if Rev. Wood might consider SEIU guilty of sin because of their capitalistic tendencies to organize as many workers as possible with one true aim in mind—collecting dues to support various political agendas. SEIU certainly appeared to me, and to many others, as a capitalistic business operation with profit motives (despite being a non-profit entity), hidden behind their cloak of solidarity and unionism. Otherwise, how could Stern earn more than a quarter of a million dollars a year, borrow 80 million dollars to buy a downtown Washington D.C. office building for it's headquarters, and spend more than 80 million dollars of members' dues during the 2008 election on political candidates sympathetic to his cause, while at the same time underfunding members' employee benefit plans?

Speaking, it appeared, to folks like me who fought back against the union movement where its intent was questionable at best, Rev. Wood wrote, "It has become commonplace for companies, large and small, to hire union-busting consultants whenever their employees begin to show an interest in joining a union." I was innocent of these charges as I had no intention of busting any union but simply wanted my workers to know the true facts and be able to decide whether they wanted to be organized through the time-tested and time-honored secret-ballot election. In fact, on several occasions I had requested both the union and the clergy group to petition the NLRB for a secret-ballot election. Their response—it takes too long to have an election and it is weighted too heavily in favor of the company. This belief exists despite statistics indicating that unions win more than 50 percent of such elections. But this is not good enough for Stern or Rev. Wood. They want to win 100 percent of the time by having the company sign a Neutrality Agreement, or by getting the EFCA passed. What the workers want is incidental to the SEIU agenda.

I did agree with Rev. Wood's conclusion that "labor unions also run the potential of becoming idols. When they lose sight of how their interests contribute to the common good, when their internal procedures stifle participatory democracy, when an elite and self-serving leadership perpetuates corruption, then the union becomes an idol that truncates the image of God in their members." To this, and his words, "This is the sin of the labor organizer's situation. The organizer is tempted to perpetuate this sinful context by using people, concocting half-truths, and seeking quick gains in the name of helping the cause," I simply said, "Amen" as this described the conduct of the SEIU and Stern to a "T."

Another statement Rev. Wood made in his 2004 book resonated with me as I tried to assess the validity of my new adversary: "In many cases, the only thing restraining the wickedness of a corporation is a labor union." While this may be true of some companies, I felt that if I could show Rev. Wood this was completely false at EMS, perhaps he would understand my reluctance to bow to SEIU demands. Demands truly targeted at, to use his words, stifling "participatory democracy."

Adding Rev. Cushman Wood, the Interfaith Worker Justice, and the Indianapolis Clergy Committee to the mix meant my opponents on the battlefield were growing by the day. When my head hit the pillow at night, my mind was a twisted mess trying to keep track of all the brushfires burning as the union stepped up its game plan to destroy EMS's reputation, forcing us to agree to the Neutrality Agreement. Sometimes, I hoped that I might wake up and realize the war had just been part of a bad dream. But this wasn't to be as each day presented a new challenge.

By mid-April, the SEIU targeted the Sallie Mae building in Indianapolis. Reports reached me that between 7 and 9 a.m., several organizers appeared on the street distributing flyers stating that EMS "Keeps Janitors in Poverty." Their efforts stopped rush-hour traffic, causing me to decide that a meeting with Rev. Wood might be in order. Certainly, I was anxious to meet this man who was so concerned with social justice yet backed a union like the SEIU—one that didn't appear to give a damn about it.

On April 23, 2007, I held a meeting with Rev. Wood, Rev. C. J. Hawking, Sister Mary Ann, Father Tom Fox, and Rev. Linda McCrae along with my daughter Kelly, head of human resources at EMS. Rev. Woods began the discussion by saying that he understood, based on his meeting with one of our customers, that I was willing to remain neutral regarding unionization. I said that was true and that we had encouraged the SEIU to petition for a secret-ballot election with the NLRB.

Rev. Woods then proceeded to inform me that their definition of neutral was for me to sign a Neutrality Agreement. Things then tensed up a bit, especially after I made it clear there was no intention on my part to sign the Agreement. This did not win me any friends in the building. As blank faces greeted every word, I told the clergy my true feelings. Because EMS currently paid above-average industry wages along with medical and dental benefits, holiday pay and vacation time—wages and benefits better than the union negotiated in Cincinnati, it was not in the best interest of our employees for me to sign the Agreement, especially when it was not morally right for me to make their decision for them.

Forging ahead, I used the example of St. Louis unionized workers. They currently were paid 6 dollars and 75 cents per hour, well below our wage pay scale of nearly eight dollars per hour. I also emphasized that union members were required to pay as much as 40 dollars a month in union dues, decreasing their take home pay. When the argument was offered about workers being subject to "revolving door" policies based on large turnover, I attempted to discuss certain employees at EMS who had made false accusations about their work status. But the clergy did not want to hear about them, and I was diverted into explaining how the average tenure for an EMS worker was 2 years and that many jobs were designed to supplement income—part-time. The union never mentioned much about this, but I thought it an important point because we were proud of those who picked up some extra income by working a few hours a week. They were just as important to us as our full-time employees especially as many worked with short notice when a client needed a building or plant cleaned because of an emergency.

The discussion became rather heated when Rev. Hawking wondered why I would not sign the Neutrality Agreement. My explanation that doing so would give up the employee's right to a secret-ballot election appeared to fall on deaf ears, and I was chastised for not being a "leader." Attempting to keep my composure in light of jabs at my character, we moved on to Rev. Wood's concerns about what information was being provided to the workers by both EMS and the union. Once that subject was debated and re-debated with my explaining how the union appeared to be less interested in workers knowing all the facts, a tense atmosphere began to permeate the room when Rev. Hawking suddenly exclaimed, "[I] received a call from [a] Sallie Mae [executive] to let me know that they would no longer be using EMS's services because EMS would not recognize the union." When I mentioned that was not the information I received, she boldly replied, "Are you calling me a liar?" Regrouping, I denied this, but expressed disbelief that Sallie Mae had made such a claim as I knew their executive would not make such an assertion. To bolster her argument that the call had been received and its substance correctly interrupted, Rev. Hawking said that she had a voice mail on her cell phone from the executive confirming the company's intention to dump EMS because we were non-union. Before I could ask to hear it, Rev. Wood announced that he had to leave. As a parting comment, he said he did not care if SEIU was a "less than forthright organization" as he believed in what unions could do for people. I looked at Kelly and she looked at me as we were both thinking, "What?" Before I could ask him his meaning, he asked if I was going to be a "leader" by signing the Neutrality Agreement, and when I said "No," he said, "You are obviously anti-union and I am pro-union and I have more important things to do." He shook my hand and left.

Later, in the meeting with the clergy, a moment occurred that still seems unreal. Father Tom Fox, a Franciscan priest working in the Hispanic ministry for the Archdiocese of Indianapolis made a telling comment. A caring man, he was over a year later described in a newspaper article as a "saint" by one admirer. When a reporter called for an interview, I even added a nice compliment to the mix as I respected the man, despite disagreeing with him about many union issues and his comment on this day.

Comparisons were being made between the wages that janitors earned in Indianapolis and Cincinnati; I pointed out an apparent discrepancy—that our workers were making more money per hour and had access to better benefits than union workers in Ohio. Father Fox then spoke up and said, "David, please understand, we don't care about the facts. All we care about is that unions lift people out of poverty and we want you to be union." This was disturbing as I knew full well that those workers in Cincinnati were being hoodwinked by savvy union language promising higher wages but also containing omissions about union dues payments reducing the take-home pay. These workers were also told about better benefits not realizing that most didn't kick into being until three years after the signing of any agreement and only if an employee worked full-time for at least six months. Because many union employees still only work part-time despite supposed gains, they would never be eligible for such benefits. This is because although the union differentiated between full- and part-time (full time 35 hours versus 30 hours for EMS employees), the union contracts contained out-clauses where the building owners or managers could set working hours because of energy or security concerns. When they did so, they were often the same hours. Therefore, the facts didn't fit the impressive statements of up to 150 percent improvement in take-home-pay the clergy proposed as the reason for lauding the union for saving workers from so-called poverty situations. It was thus clear that these clergy did not understand at all the factual evidence in the union contracts. Worse still, apparently they did not care.

Another tense moment occurred when I asked if the clergy's congregations were aware and approved of their work and position on this issue. I was told in no uncertain terms by several members of the group that it was not their congregation's concern or decision. I then asked again if it wasn't important to make sure they had the facts. Linda McCrae who was sitting next to my daughter said they did not need to know the facts as they were busy people. Kelly nearly jumped out of her seat at that point but I restrained her before she could act. Thank goodness I had told her to let me do the talking at the meeting. Otherwise, the outcome of the meeting might have been worse than it was.

Kelly probably could describe my facial expression better than me, but I am sure I was blank-faced for what seemed like five minutes. In fact, I wondered if I had really heard Father Fox and Linda's words correctly, but after a moment's thought, I realized I had. Because I didn't want to cause a scene, we moved on to other subjects but the words spoken resonated in my confused mind for sometime to come. If he and Linda, and others like Rev. Wood, didn't care about the facts, then what could be done?

After some talk about various wage scales for workers both in our industry and others, I asked Rev. Hawking about the voice mail message she had mentioned. She finally agreed to let me listen, and when I did, there was nothing in the message about Sallie Mae canceling our business. Rev. Hawking backtracked a bit, but it was clear to me and the others that she had exaggerated her communication with the Sallie Mae executive. Considering the deception later, it disturbed me that someone like Rev. Hawking was providing others with false facts inflaming an already delicate situation. The old adage, "the truth shall set you free," is still a tried and true staple and I was convinced that if I could simply help people like these clergy understand the facts, they would soon soften their position regarding their support for the SEIU. Despite my efforts, such a blessing never occurred.

Later, when we asked the Sallie Mae executive whether EMS lost the Sallie Mae account because we were not union, she denied it as well as making any statement to that effect to Rev. Hawking. Instead, the account changed cleaning contractors because of a "nationwide contract decision" having nothing to do with the SEIU–EMS stalemate. It was all price-related. She thanked us for our 16-year business relationship and wished us nothing but the best.

As the calendar turned to late April, another EMS customer, The Children's Museum, was subject to union activity. A van approached the building full of union organizers. They passed out flyers and posted one on the customer's bulletin board. On April 27, protesters banging buckets to make themselves noticed collected at the corner of Market and Illinois streets before police responded and broke up the rally.

On the first day of May, union organizers in purple shirts bearing flyers with the headline, "Try Your Fortune On $45 A Day," appeared in quick succession at Market Tower, Indianapolis Power and Light, and in front of the Guaranty Building. Featured on the flyer was a full paragraph of accusations by "Sadie–EMS Janitor." She alleged that when she "got sick and had to miss days because I was in the hospital, EMS fired me." Such statements hurt me deeply as this was not at all what had occurred, and she knew it. Seeing people like Sadie being used by SEIU made me want to strike out with every bit of energy I had to stop the madness. But I knew Stern and his union buddies would welcome such behavior and I had to swallow my tongue and do my fighting in other ways.

Just when I thought things might calm down, they got worse. On May 2, someone at SEIU had quite a novel idea. Fifteen or so organizers strode into the Market Tower lobby and released several hundred purple and yellow helium balloons imprinted with "Justice for Janitors." Beating on drums and chanting accompanied the surge as the balloons floated to the ceiling of the four-story atrium.

As I sat alone in my office and tried to comprehend what was occurring, I lowered my head into my hands and prayed that such incidents would cease. I hated it that my customers were being subjected to the harassment and would have understood perfectly if they had called and canceled our contracts. But so far, with the exception of businesses such as Lilly and Wellpoint that would not even let us bid on contracts for fear of reprisals and bad public relations, our customer base stayed firm.

Because the tactics employed thus far were obtaining minimal results, if any, SEIU organizers began getting personal about convincing our employees they better become union members. On May 4, a security officer at Market Tower reported an "older white woman with a green blouse and black pants with long blondish hair . . . jumping out of her car when EMS employees were walking into the building." When the employees were reluctant to speak, the woman offered them five dollars to listen. After the woman grabbed one employee's arm, police were called. When they arrived, the protesters were asked to sit down and names were taken. A few days later, another incident occurred and police told protesters they would be arrested if they returned.

One of the women accosted was a 55-year-old employee named Mary. She worked hard and we valued her as a worker. But her age and frailty didn't concern the organizers who offered her five bucks to listen to union propaganda and to sign a union card. They were bullies and knew Mary could easily be influenced and intimidated. Despite her repeated refusals to sign a union card over the next four months—asking for police help and private escort to her car—she finally broke down, signed their card, and went on strike for them. What a pity as this kindly woman, paid by the union while she was on strike, was then cast away like a rag doll later when they were through using her. Bullies caused Mary to lose a good job complete with benefits. She was a true victim of the war. We had actually filed charges against the SEIU alleging they had harassed and intimidated our employees including Mary, but the charges were dismissed because the employees were afraid to come forward during the investigation. We later learned that the NLRB actually had documented knowledge of her harassment by the SEIU based upon an affidavit she gave during their investigations of the SEIU's charges against EMS. Despite these obvious facts, the NLRB could not or would not put two and two together and protect Mary, which was their primary job. The war continued to escalate on several fronts, especially in Cincinnati where flyers were handed out at a customer's building. A new tactic emerged, SEIU chastised the insurance company for charging policyholders higher insurance premiums "just because of their race." Injecting the race card shocked me, as did the inference in the flyer that the company used a cleaning company where "most of the [workers] are African-American," implying EMS was guilty of some sort of racial discrimination as one that paid "poverty wages."

Continuing the attack on all fronts, SEIU sent a scathing letter to one of our large Indianapolis customers alleging that we refused "to agree to a process to turn positions into good jobs with health care," a reference to the union's implication that we were the bad guys preventing the city's janitors the "ability to compete for good jobs in the future." In fact, our positive response to workers' needs to the tune of better than average wages, health care, and benefits was squarely in line with promoting an atmosphere where our company could compete for good jobs in the future. Fortunately, they understood and knew the true EMS and did not buy into the union propaganda.

As the criticism and the protests piled on, sometimes by the end of a workday, I wanted to escape to Mars where I could find some relief from the tension and the conflict. But as commander-in-chief of our troops, there was no time for such things—new challenges arose every time I picked up the telephone, read an e-mail or newspaper, or perused a letter telling me of yet another union incident. Barb was my comfort during these times as she always had been along with members of my family and friends both at home and at the office. All were encouraging, all kept telling me to keep the faith, that if nothing else, we would outlast Stern and the SEIU. But some days I wondered if they would ever quit despite our efforts to the contrary.

On the morning of May 11, I learned of potential violence occurring the night before when SEIU organizers prevented EMS female workers outside Market Tower from entering their cars. Money was once again offered if the scared employees would listen. When the workers tried to leave, they were prevented from doing so. Police were called and the employees had to be escorted to their cars. How long would it be, I feared, before someone overreacted and blood was spilled? How I prayed this would never happen.

Seven days later, an arrest was finally necessary when Rev. Cushman Wood led a group of about 40 protesters as they marched down the street toward Market Tower singing, "We Shall Overcome." When they "camped" in the lobby, a police warning was issued to six clergy, including Father Tom Fox; they were arrested. *The Indianapolis Star* reporter indicated, "The arrests were a dramatic escalation of protests that have gone on for more than two years in Indianapolis on behalf of janitors." Rev. Wood, after stating that EMS was the culprit as we had "rebuffed" SEIU's plan to unionize, was quoted as saying, "What's going on in Indianapolis is economic segregation. People don't have a livable wage." Thankfully, the reporter presented both sides of the story by quoting the Market Tower property manager we dealt with: "Full-time janitors who clean the building are paid better than typical union wages and offered health insurance." This was presented in one of the final paragraphs of the article, one titled, "Going on Faith to Jail: Clergy Members Arrested," making me wonder whether anyone read our side of the story. But at least it had been printed; other media reports were as one-sided as the Detroit Lions 2008 won-loss record.

On the Sunday following the arrests, as I walked into my own church, I wondered whether fellow parishioners

"Each person is created in the image of God."

That includes EMS janitors.

Yesterday, religious leaders in Indianapolis were arrested.

Why? They wanted us to hear a message: We are all created in the image of God, including low-wage janitors who work for Executive Management Services, the company hired to clean this building.

Unlike other regional cleaning companies, Indianapolis-based EMS refuses to allow its workers the freedom to choose a union and begin to lift themselves out of poverty.

Through the 'Three Cities One Future Campaign,' janitors, other service workers and community members in Cincinnati, Columbus, and Indianapolis are fighting for dignity.

EMS janitors have gained the impassioned support of clergy members.

Now they need yours.

For more information, visit www.threecitiesonefuture.org.

SEIU
THREE CITIES ONE FUTURE
CINCINNATI | COLUMBUS | INDIANAPOLIS

questioned my defiant attitude toward the union. Was God on the side of the workers and was I being a Judas-like foil, a traitor to their rights, a less-than-caring corporate figurehead whose only god was the almighty dollar? No one said anything, but as I looked around, I hoped people understood my position and that in reality, I was being an advocate for the employees not their enemy. How I hoped they knew me well enough that I could continue to have their respect. One reason I believed this was possible had been the supporting words of our pastor whom I had spoken to on several occasions about the situation. I knew he was in our corner as were many parishioners who were aware of the situation and the one-sided stories in the press.

Hoping to present our side of the facts once again, I had sent a two-page letter to clergy members stressing my desire to "be sure that you have the full story about EMS and that you know the truth about the union you are supporting." I then detailed the advantages workers enjoyed at EMS, while discounting any perspective that we did not respect employee rights. I also hit the objections I had to the Neutrality Agreement and pointed to an incident where workers in Oregon had filed charges with the NLRB that "the union [SEIU] used outdated cards in order to secure representation without an election" in violation of the secret ballot provisions and even the card check process. When several smaller SEIU locals in California merged, I noted, workers had to reapply for jobs, take pay cuts, and do one year's probation while quoting the California Local SEIU President who said, "I'm ashamed to say that I am a member of SEIU." Closing, I reminded the clergy of SEIU's relentless and ruthless campaign against EMS and the filing of several frivolous claims with the NLRB while stating once again my support for secret-ballot elections as provided by law. Whether these words changed anyone's mind I did not know, but whenever a chance appeared to tell our story, I took advantage of the opportunity. More than anything though I was careful not to lower myself, or EMS, to the SEIU's level and disparage them with cutting remarks cast out when I was upset. I wanted EMS to always be above the fray and be professional; a goal I believe we accomplished every step of the way.

Regardless, during the early part of June, EMS was peppered from all sides with NLRB charges, OSHA charges and then flyers, handbills, letters and faxes to clients, protests, and demonstrations, all portraying our company as the evil dragon trying to suppress employee rights. One flyer left at Indianapolis Power & Light read in part: "IPL SEE THE LIGHT," "Civil Rights and Freedom of Speech stomped at EMS account – Janitors Press For Investigation." What investigation was this? And by whom? How I would have welcomed a full-scale investigation in an objective forum. The first witness I wanted to call was Stern.

On June 12, a new tactic was pulled from the SEIU arsenal when four people claiming to be painters entered a customer's building in Cincinnati. Before their credentials could be checked, they sped up the steps before returning a few minutes later. When the building manager checked, the intruders had positioned a huge banner imprinted with the words "Western Southern Chooses Corporate Greed Over Community Need – Justice For Janitors." Hearing that word "greed" used to label both our customers, and by inference, EMS, broke my heart. Was there no end to the SEIU war to destroy everything I had worked nearly 20 years to build?

The War Rages On

"You personally ran after some employees who wanted to be organized."

When I read this e-mail from a colleague in Cincinnati, I wanted to throw my telephone through the large window glass a few feet from my desk. Was it possible someone thought I would ever do such a thing? Apparently so, as this colleague also wrote, "I have a witness for you who can say that he was told that directly by the SEIU." Thankfully my colleague would later e-mail, "My client was incensed with the mere suggestion of it. He knew it was utter garbage."

Personal stains on my reputation had become commonplace during this SEIU war, something I had never endured before. We all have egos, but this was more about simply who I was and the accusation that I would ever chase after someone who was interested in becoming involved in a labor union. Despite the pain, I had to chuckle as I tried to imagine a six-foot four-inch fellow with a bad knee galloping after a worker screaming "No union! No union! No union." With this in mind, I simply e-mailed my colleague back, "The SEIU organizers do have active imaginations."

What actually occurred was this—I was downtown for an IPL meeting and as I left the building, I noticed there was a space available for rent. As we were looking for a recruiting office, the leasing agent guided me to the elevator and then to a vacant office, one, ironically, right next to the one occupied by SEIU. Two guys, both wearing SEIU T-shirts, then appeared and told us our renting wasn't a good idea. We left that floor and went to the agent's office where I explained the situation. She agreed that EMS renting the space would not work. I left the building, and the two men fell in lockstep with me. One named John, whom I later discovered was the fiancé of Rebecca Maran, SEIU's chief organizer and manager for Indianapolis, asked what I was doing there, and when I told him it was really none of his business, he began, as did the other fellow, to berate me for my anti-union stance. This occurred for a couple of blocks or so as I attempted in every way to keep things calm. Finally, I went one way and they another. Then the e-mail arrived alleging that I had run after union organizers to chase them away. This was untrue, but even the sense that I was being followed and that I had to watch every move I made out of concern for my safety was new to my way of life. All I could do was carry on and ready myself for the next SEIU assault.

Protests and rallies where handbills and flyers were handed out, and letters sent from clergy including Rev. Wood and Rev. Hawking to customers continued through the middle of June as warmer temperatures covered the Midwest. The clergy committee's letter on June 12· once again included the names of 125 supposed supporters from different denominations. I wondered if they had read and checked the facts before they signed the document or just placed blind faith in what the SEIU told them.

On June 19, a flyer was passed out with the following information: "THIS IS IT!! Join Jobs with Justice in this nationwide RALLY in support of the EMPLOYEE FREE CHOICE ACT." Below this language were the words, "Tell Senator Lugar That YOUR rights ARE important." Along with the flyer was another titled "Employee Free Choice Act:

Ten Things to Know." Facts in support included: "American workers want to join unions. Research shows nearly 60 million would form a union tomorrow if given the chance," "Too few ever get that chance because employers routinely block their efforts," "The Employee Free Choice Act would give workers a fair chance to form unions," and "The Employee Free Choice Act would put democracy back into the workplace." Wow, while I disagreed with much of what was written, this final statement caused my brain to nearly boil over. How in the world, I wondered, can the card check procedure be more democratic than the secret ballot process when under the card check system, workers cannot vote in private like they do in general elections? If anything, the card check process is undemocratic, but the SEIU twisted the words around so as to inflame those who had no idea of EFCA's true colors.

On June 22, a demonstration was held on 7th Avenue in Pittsburgh outside one of our customer's buildings with the organizers shouting, "Hey, hey, EMS has to go." By August, following distribution of a flyer stating, "Activist Fired by EMS at Market Tower," more customer letters distorting the truth about our treatment of employees, and even a dossier had been prepared about EMS called, "The Truth About Executive Management Services: A Workers View of the Indianapolis Cleaning Contractor That is Standing in the Way of Better Jobs." Free lemonade was used to influence potential supporters when those protesting EMS set up a lemonade stand in an attempt to gain sympathy for the union cause. Additionally, they reportedly had pre-programmed cell phones with the Market Tower owner's telephone number. Supporters then flooded the line with calls clogging the voice-mail lines.

The flyers used had photographs of kids detailing how their parents worked for poverty wages and were forced to work two and three jobs to make a living. It was reprehensible to use kids to make the union point, especially when there was big screen TV in the background and the truth was that

WHAT HAPPENS AT MARKET TOWER AFTER TENANTS LEAVE FOR THE DAY?

**INTIMIDATION
FIRING OF UNION SUPPORTERS
WORKER EXPLOITATION
CIVIL RIGHTS ABUSES
THREATENED PHYSICAL
VIOLENCE**

CONTRACTORS AT MARKET TOWER ARE OUT OF CONTROL

The contractor hired to clean this building, Indianapolis-based Executive Management Services, has initiated an unprecedented attack against working families in the Midwest who are standing up for the American Dream.

Now, Market Tower security guards are routinely threatening and intimidating janitors by calling the police to prevent janitors from holding union meetings after work, engaging in surveillance against workers engaged in protected activity and threatening physical violence against union organizers.

Indianapolis janitors are fighting for a better future for their families.

END THE CIVIL RIGHTS ABUSES AND SUPPORT WORKING FAMILIES

their parents were earning higher wages at EMS than those negotiated by the union.

Realizing my temper limit was fast approaching as we continued to be bombarded by the enemy, I decided on a tactic designed to call SEIU's bluff. With assistance from my legal experts, we drafted a paid newspaper advertorial with the headline, "Dear SEIU, Please 'Fish or Cut Bait!'" Five paragraphs outlined several important aspects in our war with the union, including the opening sentence: "For several months now EMS, Inc, a local commercial cleaning firm, has been under an undeserved and relentless attack by the

Service Employees International Union (the 'SEIU'), a multi-million dollar labor union headquartered in Washington, D.C." Then we informed readers that, among other things, "EMS janitors are among the highest compensated in each of its markets." We continued, "Because the union cannot convince EMS employees that a union and its dues, fees, fines, and assessments are in their best interests, the SEIU has pressured EMS customers to stop doing business with the company," and ". . . the union is currently under investigation by the NLRB in Indianapolis and Cincinnati for these stunts." To indicate our willingness to proceed according to law, we added, "EMS is very willing to let its employees vote in a secret-ballot election conducted by the federal government to decide whether they want to be members of your union or not."

My hope was that business owners in Indianapolis and beyond would understand our position more clearly. And by stating in the final paragraph, "If our employees vote your way, you will have what you want. If our employees vote against you, please take your organizing effort to another city or group of employees who desire what you are selling," I was trying to force the union to take a stand. Of course, they did nothing as they knew if a legal secret-ballot election was held, EMS employees would send them packing.

Flyers written in Spanish were distributed by SEIU for an August 15, 2007 rally, and attendees were guaranteed purple shirts. On the chosen day, marchers began at noon at Monument Circle; two former EMS workers and several clergy spoke. In response to the allegations, we decided to fight with flyers of our own stating the EMS position. One of those handing these flyers out later reported that when he gave them to pro-union workers, they said, "This is a bunch of crap; shame on you." Chants, songs, and prayer occurred and our representative was not harmed at what was called a "Purple Rally."

One speaker apparently stood out from the rest—Rev. Cushman Wood reportedly used such words as "wicked, uncaring, and evil" to describe EMS. Another speaker was so wrapped up in his cause, he said everything being done was "God's will," and that "God was on their side." Rev. Wood's flyers indicated he and his SEIU followers were celebrating the fact that Eli Lilly, Simon Malls, Duke Realty, and Sallie Mae had "responded positively. But some businesses had not," a reference to EMS customers. Including Simon in the mix was a bit misleading as they rather skirted around the issue of endorsing SEIU; ironically, EMS was actually at one time a sub-contractor for Simon but the union did not know it.

To harass customers, a building manager's telephone number was given out, tying up phone lines and voice mail for hours on end as pressure built on a daily basis. I tried to keep calm, to assess the enemy's strategies and see whether their tactics were working. Thus far, our customers had been loyal to us, but I knew some were at the breaking point. How easy it would have been for them to ask to be released from the EMS contract. We would have done so without question but with a heavy heart as our working relationships with businesses and buildings across the country were precious to us. Even worse, we knew that when a business caved in, workers were going to be less protected, not more, as SEIU's hypocritical attitude of saying one thing and doing another meant lower wages and more costly benefits in the long run. Despite all of the flyers, handbills, demonstrations, and media attention, thus far only a handful of EMS employees out of more than 400 in Indianapolis had defected, but I could still expect a stampede to the door if the SEIU attacks on EMS employees became too intense.

Ever ready to speak with anyone on the opposition team (I was still waiting for a call from Stern), Father Tom Fox agreed to meet me for a one-on-one chat about the

EMS–SEIU stalemate. But when he began the conversation by informing me that if his father and two brothers, all businessmen including one brother, a General Motors executive, had not been able to persuade him to change his pro-union attitude, I "certainly was not going to." I knew we were headed for an uphill battle. I explained that I wasn't trying to sway him from his pro-union stance but wanted him to know all of the facts involved. He replied with suggestions that elections took too long under the present secret ballot system and I countered by explaining that nearly a year had passed since I offered to have an election. Within that time, we could have had eight or nine elections! Then he said we "brainwashed, intimidated, and harassed" workers. I told him that was not our way and he was welcome to talk to some of our employees if he wished to do so. He brought up the names of two men who had complained, and I told him to talk to the 34 on that crew who had not. When the meeting ended, we agreed to disagree and that was that, with my hope that our meeting might cool down the escalating war.

But it didn't. On September 25, I received a fax with the following message:

. . . .

Dear David Bego,

We are writing to inform you that EMS employees at 10 W. Market St. and SkyBank, as of September 25, 2007 are participating in an unfair labor practice strike until further notice. They are protesting charges of unfair labor practices including those described in NLRB cases: (case numbers followed)

Sincerely,
Rebecca Maran

. . . .

Scattered to the right and above her name (she was the SEIU Local 3 representative) were the written names of seven employees. Yes, it was true—for the first time in its

04/25/2007

nearly 20-year history—EMS employees were striking. What a sad day this was, one I would never forget.

Of immediate concern was someone to clean the buildings affected by the strikers. To my sincere appreciation, management, clerical employees, and employees from other buildings rose to the occasion and volunteered to work until we had the workers replaced. Then we set about finding new employees who would be willing to work even though the union was picketing every night in front of the building. Kelly worked hard to select the proper people, including one EMS employee who asked to come back to work right after the strike actually began, saying she did not agree with the union. One of our human resources people who substituted found out what union pressure was all about when he was approached by an organizer who told him, "We'll pay you your normal wages if you stay out here on strike with us." When the EMS employee said he wasn't interested, the organizer promised him higher wages and better benefits with the union, noting that EMS's current pay package was F*ck*ng B*ll Sh*t! If the strike caused me to lose my breath, then a second incident quickly reminded me once again of the potential for violence, my worst nightmare. This occurred when a "short blond [SEIU] organizer" grabbed an EMS supervisor named Lucy while she was trying to enter Market Tower. She said, "Don't go in there. Take that shirt off and put this one on [purple SEIU shirt]. We will pay you for today. They can't fire you." Fortunately Lucy did not retaliate and entered the building, but I feared more of these incidents could occur and at some point tempers would boil to the point of no return.

If fighting the Christian brothers and sisters supporting SEIU was not hard enough, two days before the end of September, the CEO of an Indianapolis-based company, received a threatening letter from the Islamic Society of North America. Signed by Secretary General Muneer Fareed, the letter expressed reservations about an industry "plagued with low wages, discrimination, and health and safety concerns." Specifically, Fareed stated "As Muslims of faith we find the current treatment of these workers to be reprehensible," before alerting the CEO that "we are aware that your company is in the process of opening a Shariah-compliant fund on the London and Dubai stock exchange. Should the situation at the buildings in Indianapolis not come to a swift and just resolution, we will continue with our campaign to inform your investors and the worldwide Muslim community of this urgent and unacceptable state of affairs."

In an effort to apply even more pressure, the SEIU sent one of the disgruntled EMS employees to London so she could picket at an Islamic Economic Conference. The aim: to embarrass the owners of Market Tower and disrupt the proceedings. We discovered this when London's *Guardian* newspaper called me for an interview. News accounts also appeared in the *Irish Times* triggering global coverage of our union battle.

For those unfamiliar with union tactics, a threatening letter from an organization like the Islamic Society seems unreal. But this sort of behavior is commonplace when a win-at-all-cost attitude prevails like it does at SEIU. Certainly Stern and his cohorts believed the ends justified the means even if the means meant spreading untruths when the truth was known. Or bringing into the fight the Islamic Society, despite their leaders having little or no idea of the background causing the strife between EMS and SEIU. Regardless, now the war had stretched across the Atlantic where a valued customer was being assaulted for its association with EMS. Were there no lengths to which SEIU would go to win? Were there no depths to which Stern and the union would stoop to get their way? Poor Gerald, I thought. I can't even imagine what his reaction must have been to receiving this letter. I'm sorry, I thought. I really am.

Interestingly enough I later learned that a scholar from the Middle East fund visited the Islamic Society in Indiana and discussed the situation with them and they realized they were being manipulated to use religious sympathies based on groundless facts.

While I tried to be active at every turn as new developments occurred almost hourly, an October 1-fax from Rebecca Maran reported that unnamed EMS employees at two other buildings had joined the strikers. The next day, a fax signed by 14 EMS Indianapolis employees was sent to EMS customers in Cincinnati explaining their decision to strike in Indianapolis. The text above the signatures stated, "While the janitorial industry moves forward, EMS chooses to move backwards . . . We desire to have pride in our jobs and do the best work possible for our tenants . . . But how can that happen while we work in a volatile and hostile workplace lacking benefits and earning wages that leave our families in poverty?"

As I read these words, I wondered if I had been too stubborn, too set in my ways. Had I really listened well enough to employee concerns over the years? Was I truly backward with my thinking? Was the SEIU the saving grace these workers believed it to be? Was I standing in the way of worker progress? Should I pick up the telephone and call Stern, and say, "Okay, I have seen the light. I'll sign the Neutrality Agreement?" No, I couldn't do that as it wasn't a matter of winning or losing, or perhaps even who was right and who was wrong, but my strong belief that the SEIU was hoodwinking workers into believing they could better their plight in life through unionization, if only they would give up their right to secret-ballot elections. I couldn't let that happen. Even though I had asked several times for the union to show me how this was possible, they never once had done so. With new resolve, I decided to stay the course, absorb the abuse, put up with the strikers, and perhaps decide to take some bolder action toward an offensive of some sort designed to counterattack SEIU like they had never been counterattacked before. How I might do that was unclear, but my mind was swirling around some thoughts about a potential course of action.

At this point I knew the union was getting desperate and the strike was proof positive; it was really the last gasp effort of its failing Corporate Campaign against EMS. Above all, it was important to remember that the union is a business and it has a business plan when it enters a metropolitan area to organize. Experiences in Cincinnati and Houston told us that the union wanted to wrap things up in a two-year time period and it was fast approaching two years since GSF became the first signatory to a Neutrality Agreement in Indianapolis in December of 2005. We figured if we could last until the end of December, the pressure would subside. We also were encouraged by the fact that so few EMS employees had joined the strike meaning the workers were not buying what the union was selling. I salute our savvy employees for the wisdom to see through the baloney being fed them. What we needed now was to stick a sword in the SEIU heart to kill the beast threatening us at every turn.

We had filed several charges in early May with the NLRB against the SEIU for employee harassment but those charges were later dismissed because the employees who had complained were reluctant to come forward for fear of retaliation by the SEIU. While the SEIU swears the board favors businesses, this could not be further from the truth as facts indicate that time and time again, the NLRB prosecutes more charges against employers than it does against unions. This will be even more apparent now that President Obama has nominated a former SEIU attorney to the board. How objective do you think he will be if confirmed?

In any event, we decided it was time to put both the SEIU and the NLRB on the spot for the union's continued employee harassment and intimidation, as well as violations of the National Labor Relations Act (NLRA). The plan we had in mind was militaristic in nature, one where we would strike with overwhelming firepower.

As we plotted our strategy, another employee meeting was held at Market Tower. When I rose to speak and looked into the faces of employees who had worked for us for years with no hint of discontent, I could not help but become emotional. Big guys like me aren't supposed to show such feelings, but I truly did love these people and wanted the best for them. Unlike me, they had never been able to enjoy some of the sweeter parts of life, especially education, the strong foundation for job advancement. Without it, there is less chance of growth, and fewer alternatives available other than hourly wage jobs. But none of these people I knew were gripers; nobody was blaming anyone else for their inability to earn more. All I could do was be fair to these hardworking men and women and look out for their best interests. Some, like the SEIU, wanted to paint me as the evil one, but I cared and nothing was going to change that attitude.

I began my speech by telling the workers the purpose of the meeting was to discuss recent and past events concerning this battle between EMS and the union. I made it clear that any decision to organize was *their* decision, one guaranteed to them under federal law. Realizing they wondered if any of the allegations against me were true, I emphasized that neither I nor any of the managers had or were going to harass, intimidate, or take action against any of them if they were pro-union. We would operate, I explained, within the law and if any instance of foul play by our management team occurred, they should immediately contact human resources. Then I laid out 11 different "true facts" for them to consider touching on subjects ranging from whom SEIU was, to their organizational intentions in the "Tri-city campaign," to the Neutrality Agreement and its potential impact, to the union being a business and mostly interested in union dues, and finally to the fact that Interfaith Worker Justice had been supported by SEIU to the tune of one hundred thousand dollars in donations for the two previous years. Hopefully, this provided our employees with both sides of the story, my only intention.

When the striking employees requested their paychecks, we gave them out without so much as a whimper. Yet, the union filed a charge with the NLRB alleging that we paid them one day late, an untruth. It was yet another opportunity for the union to defame EMS in a flyer. A few days later, while speaking to an International Facility Management Association (IFMA) group in Indianapolis on the subject of illegal immigration, a woman named Sarah (a striking EMS employee) interrupted by raising her hand to ask a question. Instead of directing it to the message being conveyed, she criticized EMS for low wages and no health care. I explained this was not true; IMFA officials then intervened and escorted the woman from the room. If her goal was to embarrass me, she did not do so, but I knew SEIU was shadowing every move I made, morning to night. They also had several picketers appear outside the building where I spoke, but they left before I did.

Later, we discovered the woman who had spoken out was not really one named Sarah but another, Sharon, whom the SEIU asked to impersonate Sarah when Sarah could not appear. This was the same woman the SEIU had sent to London to embarrass the owners of Market Tower. Even more interesting was that she indicated the strike was due to economic reasons and not unfair labor practices as the union claimed. We also soon realized the union had purposely set traps for our managers by having button days and other special days to trip our supervisors and managers into making mistakes so they could claim harassment and file unfair labor charges to justify the strike and tell the employees that because it was an unfair labor practice strike, they could always get their jobs back. Our supervisors and managers really did a good job of remembering their training and performed admirably! Interestingly enough, one of the SEIU organizers told one of the strikers they did not really have a good enough case for the strike, but they were desperate and running out of time and needed to move ahead!

On October 10, a noisy rally outside Market Tower by several strikers occurred. They were armed with signs stating, "EMS Workers on Strike." This occurred while supporters, dressed in purple T-shirts, handed out flyers at the Children's Museum and the Guaranty Building where they visited several businesses including The South Bend Chocolate Company and Au Bon Pain as well as the fifth-floor Arts Council. A week later, organizers at Market Tower accosted an EMS employee named Audrey. They told her to "stop being a rat and taking other people's jobs." On her report, she noted, "I felt very intimidated."

On October 22, 2007, I met with Senator Bayh's Chief of Staff at Market Tower to address his uninformed support of the SEIU. Upon my arrival, I saw a mock up of a jail cell outside of the main doors with a person inside wearing an EMS-type uniform. Picketers handed out flyers, one imprinted with the catchy words "EMS Poverty Prison." Other strikers used bullhorns to express their frustrations. On October 25, another march took place with streets closed for nearly five hours. All the while, EMS employees were stopped while walking to and from work by union organizers, many of whom made threatening gestures. One flyer used by the strikers and other protesters stated, "Tour Indianapolis Houses of Horrors" alleging "EMS Janitor who works with blood and dangerous chemicals at the pharmaceutical labs reports never having mandatory HPV vaccines [and] protective clothing. . . ."

The allegations at the pharmaceutical company for unsafe handling of chemicals really rubbed me the wrong way. I was suspicious of the source of the charges and some investigation threw a new light on what had occurred. We discovered the name of the EMS employee who submitted the claim was spelled incorrectly on the form, and that the signature did not match the one written when the employee applied for a job with us. This disclosure led us to believe the name had been forged, but we let it pass as the charges were later dismissed without question.

October 31, Halloween, certainly was an evening of ghosts and goblins for the neighbors who lived near one of my good customers Gerald Donaldson, and me. But even more for Gerald's wife. When I arrived home around 6:30 p.m. to take care of neighborhood "trick or treaters," I received a call from her. To my amazement, she told me two young children had just appeared at her door in costume asking for candy while also handing her a flyer defaming Gerald's company and EMS. My face reddened at the audacity of the union, but I tried to be calm and decide what the best course of action was.

When I stepped into our driveway, standing in front of me were the two cute little kids she had described—a boy and a girl. After giving them candy, I noticed the girl had flyers in her hand. I asked her if she was supposed to give them to me, and she said "yes," and handed me one. You could tell she was uncomfortable, poor thing.

When I looked up, there was the SEIU organizer John and a woman who looked like Becky Maran standing across the street watching the proceedings. I thanked the kids and sent them on their way. At that moment, the local police

Why Is Market Tower A Houses of Horrors For EMS Janitors?

Janitors who clean Market Tower and other prominent Indy Buildings for EMS face unsafe working conditions, broken cleaning equipment, and Management acts of intimidation and retaliation for standing up for their rights.

EMS Labor Law Violations include: Threatening, Retaliating, and Firing Workers for standing up for their rights.

"When you earn $312 every two weeks, its not enough but you still rely on your salary to provide for your family. Then the company threatens you for speaking out and fires your co-workers for speaking out. -Shaneka Brown EMS Janitor

An EMS Janitor who works with blood & dangerous chemicals at the report never having mandatory HPB vaccines, protective clothing and only had a training on safety After he complained to OSHA.

Every night is SCARY for an EMS Janitor.

Dispute with EMS and no other employer. Janitors are on strike for unfair labor practices

arrived and had the interlopers leave the neighborhood. The incident certainly showed how far the SEIU would go to win. It is a dangerous union, one that used innocent young children as pawns in their plan just as they used disgruntled and easily intimidated workers as part of their unscrupulous scheme. "Win at all cost" – that should be the SEIU motto.

Just a week or so later, on November 8, an e-mail from Gerald was an eye-opener. Through the months, he had been a staunch ally, one as loyal as a brother to me. But from the gist of his words, I could tell Gerald had just about reached his limit with SEIU tactics. In mid-October, he had agreed to meet with clergy backing the union, but that meeting did not prevent demonstrations at his home—meaning the SEIU was not only writing letters to customers, confronting them at their places of business, but was now invading their privacy by locating and demonstrating outside their homes.

Based on the upsurge in union pressure and the fact that it had become "personal," Gerald wrote, "This is getting to be difficult . . . I had no idea they would stoop to this level. I agree with your stance and I hate to see them get away with this type of action. Unfortunately, I have a responsibility to my investors which I am being reminded of more and more." Closing the message, he added, "I am not sure what our next step will be," providing me with a heads-up that he was about ready to say enough was enough, and drop us as their cleaning source. If he did so, would others follow causing a domino effect? Was the union on the brink of winning the war?

While I awaited Gerald's response, letters to customers attacking EMS grew in their ferocity. Almost every one alluded to the NLRB filings, ones stating 1) EMS illegally threatened to fire janitors participating in efforts to form a union; 2) EMS illegally threatened the loss of janitors' jobs if they choose to form a union; 3) EMS illegally threatened surveillance of janitors because they were supportive of the union; and 4) EMS illegally interrogated janitors because they were supportive of the union. Similar charges had been filed against other union holdouts, including Corporate Cleaning Systems and QBM. We noticed several similarities among the complaints indicating a cookie-cutter procedure by SEIU against those who supposedly thumbed their noses at union organizing.

At CCS, they also discovered later that the employee was a paid SEIU operative "salted" into the work force to be disruptive. Although our suspicion was we had similar occurrences at EMS, we had no proof of this. However, we did have one fellow called Daniel who ended up becoming a leader in the pro-union movement. We had problems with him not showing up for work on a consistent basis and with work performance to the extent that our customer asked us to remove him from the building. Instead of firing Daniel, we moved him to Market Tower to give him a second chance. But his attendance and performance did not improve. When a *Bible* was reported stolen from an office, he admitted stealing it and we had no choice but to terminate him. This was tough to do because Daniel had a wife and seven children with another on the way. After he was fired, the SEIU filed an NLRB complaint against us, but the union later withdrew it for lack of validity. Daniel and others like him, including an older gentleman named Hank, were easy prey for the SEIU and valuable because they provided secret information about EMS operations. Because we didn't have anything to hide, the information was basically worthless.

Every time I read the list of allegations (never accusations), my blood pressure jumped into the danger zone despite the fact that eventually virtually every single allegation filed against EMS would be reconciled in our favor. Why? Because we had documentation proving our contentions and credible witnesses to account for what had actually happened.

Nevertheless, as I sat at my desk pondering what to do next, I realized none of these charges would be reconciled for months as the slow process continued through the NLRB hearing schedules. Meanwhile, EMS was being tortured with a thousand little cuts as one union observer had stated it. Punch after punch was being thrown at me and our company and, like a fighter who feels he better start throwing some punches of his own, I decided it was time to mount the full-out, full-blown blitzkrieg-like attack we had been working on since early October. Believing those who say the best defense is many times an overwhelming offense, I called my legal experts and together we finalized our strategy designed to hit Stern and the SEIU square on the jaw with the hope we might well discover the knockout punch necessary to make them leave me, EMS, my customers, and most importantly, our employees, alone. Timing was important, I knew, because with the end of the year approaching marking the two-year point of the campaign to make us buckle under and surrender, SEIU was under the gun to produce a signed Neutrality Agreement immediately, if not sooner. We knew this based on some documentation we discovered regarding the union campaign and its plans to spend up to 2 years attempting to unionize a company before moving on. The clock was now ticking on 2 years, one second at a time.

In spite of the fact that we were holding our own, it was time to launch a guided missile. Our weapon was to file 33 separate unfair labor practice charges, all based upon documented violations of law, against SEIU with the NLRB. And to do it with flair through an accompanying press release detailing exactly those charges for everyone to see. With this game plan in tow, at 9:00 a.m. on November 14, 2007, the media were advised of our intentions in a release titled, "Service Employees International Union (SEIU) Under Investigation for Multiple Labor Law Violations." Just as Stern and the SEIU had sizzled me with allegations, we now turned the tables on them by doing the same thing. To emphasize the validity of the charges, we used a quote of mine: "We respect our employee's rights under the law, including their right not be represented by a union if that is their choice. That is not a decision that either this company or the SEIU is going to make for our employees. EMS has repeatedly asked the union to agree to a secret-ballot election conducted by the NLRB, but the union refuses to hold an election." Below this statement, we listed in summary several of our charges, including engaging in mass picketing and protests, releasing balloons, threatening to interfere with business investors unless customers agree to use a union contractor, threatening and intimidating employees, "trick or treating" at the home of an EMS customer, sending numerous letters to building owners and tenants making maliciously false and misleading statements, and conducting multiple protests and rallies against EMS without filing a petition for an NLRB election as required by federal law.

Emphasizing our position, the release closed with two important points. First, I was quoted: "The union's claim that EMS keeps janitors in poverty is absurd. We pay our janitors a higher starting wage than the union-represented janitors in Cincinnati, plus we offer health care to our full-time workers. And we offer these wages and benefits without requiring our employees to pay about $40 per month in union dues." Second, we noted, "The SEIU has come under scrutiny for its campaign tactics of harassment and intimidation in other locations as well. Last week, Wackenhut Corporation, a leading provider of security services throughout the United States, filed a lawsuit in federal court in New York City alleging racketeering and extortion by the SEIU in violation of the federal RICO laws in connection with a similar organizing campaign."

Covering eight pages, the press release then listed the 33 charges with summary details. Anyone who read them would be well aware of the ruthless campaign waged against a company whose track record with employees was exemplary. How I wanted to deliver the press release personally to Stern, Dingow, Hanrahan, Rev. Cushman Wood, Rev. C. J. Hawking, and Father Tom Fox. "Take this," I would have said while walking away with a smile on my face.

Someone said timing is everything in life, and our timing with issuing the press release was superb. In fact, we were told that the very same morning we took the offensive like Patton marching through Germany, the SEIU had its own press release ready to announce that the union was commencing contract negotiations with other cleaning companies that had signed the Neutrality Agreement. But first comes first, and when we filed our press release, they withdrew theirs. Later, we learned that SEIU's local director Rebecca Maran was extremely upset her union had been scooped. When she was asked to respond by the newspaper reporter, she backpedaled a bit from her EMS accusations saying that maybe some of what we were stating was true. This was exactly what we had in mind, for now the union was finally on the defensive, having to explain itself as we had been forced to do for the past year-plus. Rebecca must have sent word to SEIU national headquarters in Washington D.C., that she needed reinforcements as we were not backing down and instead had taken the offensive with the multiple charges. This told us the union knew they were in trouble, on the wrong side of the gun barrel, and in bunker mentality. The effect was immediate—fewer union protests, fewer flyers, and fewer handbills being distributed—less activity overall. For the first time in a long time, I could actually concentrate on helping run the company. What a relief this was for those in management who had been forced to do my job as well as their own.

How I would have loved to see Stern's face when he learned of this new development. Perhaps his face turned as purple as his trademark shirt and tie. "Who is this guy?" he probably wondered. "Why won't he cave in like all of the others?"

Divine Support

DESPITE THE APPARENT SLOW-DOWN OF UNION ACTIVITY, CONCERN FOR my own personal safety and that of my family continued. During the time when the fighting was the fiercest, I had insisted ADT install surveillance cameras at our home and that of my daughter. We notified the neighborhood security force of potential trouble especially after our neighbor was harassed at his home by SEIU operatives. I've never been a gun owner, but I became one after learning how to shoot so I could defend my family if need be.

Watching my back at all times was an eerie feeling. Even when I started the car, there was a hesitation, just a brief one, as my mind considered whether someone might have planted a bomb in retaliation for my opposition to the SEIU. I hated to even think that way, but I did, and still do. But my faith in God and my belief I was standing up for truth by defending employees who could not defend themselves, caused me comfort during the rough times. And Barb was always there with me, along with our small dog with the big heart. Playing with him and feeling the love he gave me at every turn helped during the evenings when I sat alone in my home office wondering what SEIU would throw at me next. Prayer was a constant companion as I asked the Good Lord to give me the strength to continue on. Perhaps my prayers had been answered, and due to our blitzkrieg offensive, SEIU would go away into the sunset. At least I could hope they would.

Replacing striking employees cut deep into my heart and soul as the holiday season 2007 approached. With 10 employees having decided to leave their jobs, we were forced to hire new workers to meet contract obligations. What hurt most was realizing that during Thanksgiving and Christmas when people needed extra money, the striking workers would not be paid by EMS even though the union was paying them the same wages they made at EMS with no benefits to strike, but with strings attached. While I respected the worker's right to strike, I wondered if Stern and the SEIU hierarchy cared as much for employee welfare in the same way I did. This seems almost too ludicrous to consider as it was the union that was supposed to look out for them, but when I glanced into the faces of those striking, I felt sorry for them because I truly believed they were being used by the union for its own selfish purposes.

Nevertheless, our human resources person, in this case my daughter Kelly, had begun the replacement process within minutes after we were notified of the strike. And, in what I suppose is a tribute to the type of company EMS is, there were many, many to choose from, as EMS was known as a company that paid higher wages and benefits than our competitors. All Kelly had to do was check the database and, presto, she had a list of employees ready and willing to earn good wages, benefits, holiday and vacation days, if they worked for us full-time and for a subsequent period of time. One by one, after extensive background checks, we replaced the striking workers, including two more, Dana and Juan, after we received word from SEIU that they had joined the strikers. The process took most of the month of October. In all, there would be 12 on strike out of a work force of more than 400 in Indianapolis, meaning **at least 388 *had not***. Most picketed nearly every day until the weather turned sour. Then fewer and fewer showed up.

Meanwhile, a few protests and demonstrations at customer buildings continued with foghorns, the weapon of choice, as those striking screamed in anguish about the evil EMS corporate hog. Union representatives joined the strikers, as non-striking employees were confronted entering or leaving various office buildings.

On November 9, a surprise occurred when an unannounced OSHA official visited Market Tower. Our building manager was quick to request that an EMS management representative be present, and within minutes, our safety director Terry Snyder was on the scene.

Safety director, you might ask? Yes, despite SEIU claims to the contrary, EMS had then, and has now, an entire department dedicated to nothing but employee safety. In fact, we had no real choice in the matter because federal regulations were quite clear in this area—requiring us to make certain employees worked in safe environments where there was no chance of harm. Many companies in the industry do not have such safety programs, but EMS had created a program years earlier when it recognized employee safety, even in the relatively safe cleaning environment where we operated, was paramount. Also, as we grew through acquisitions across the country, some more dangerous environments meant paying even more attention to the safety issue. The solution: We hired an expert from a Fortune 500 company. His responsibility simply was, and is, to make sure all management and employees are dedicated to an injury-free work environment every day. The department has been instrumental in developing safety programs that are at the forefront of the industry. Every employee is trained in safety; we leave nothing to chance.

Despite the existence of the safety department, SEIU never mentioned this in any of its scathing letters, press releases, or flyers during their war. No, they left all this out as well as other programs we had installed specifically to benefit workers. Good news like this was not of interest to the union. They wanted to paint a bleak picture of EMS as a "rat contractor," paying poverty wages and forcing employees to work in hazardous conditions with inadequate safety equipment . All of this was part of the campaign to smear us, to make us look like a greedy, non-caring corporation, part of the dreaded corporate America only interested in multi-million-dollar profits.

As I awaited word of OSHA's inspection at Market Tower where complaints had been filed, I was confident we would pass with the proverbial flying colors. And we did, of course, because the complaints were a bunch of baloney— none of them valid in any way. The best the union could do was to point to a couple of improperly labeled bottles and a frayed extension cord, hardly earth-shattering evidence of incompetence on our part. In fact, there were never any penalties or fines imposed on EMS indicating the small nature of the complaints. But this did not keep the SEIU from sending out flyers and letters with allegations that EMS had major violations and used hazardous chemicals despite both union and non-union buildings around the country having many of the same minor violations that we experienced, and in many cases much worse.

Despite our innocence, the strike continued. Flyers imprinted with such phrases as, "Janitors On Strike," "Unfair Labor Practice Strike," and "EMS Janitors have faced threats, intimidation, surveillance, interrogation, and firing for union activity" were in view for all to see. Others stated, "EMS. Can't Take It No More" followed by a quote from an EMS employee: "EMS has gotten away with paying us next to nothing and giving us broken and sub-standard equipment." Nothing could have been further from the truth, but the union didn't care. All they wanted was to dirty our name with accusation after accusation intending to draw sympathy from customers and the media at large. How I hated for my customers to endure such a disruption, but so far they had stayed the course with me through this difficult time.

Reports of harassment and retaliation...
Reports of discrimination...
Reports of safety hazards...

If Executive Management Services Janitorial
(EMS) gave janitors a lump of coal this holiday,
it might be an improvement.

Over the last four years, local janitors and community allies with the national Justice for Janitors effort have successfully transformed contract cleaning from a poverty wage industry into an industry on the road to living wages, affordable healthcare, and greater work hours.

Executive Management Services (EMS), the cleaning contractor at this building, chooses to fight janitors instead of working with them for good jobs. EMS janitors report **Unfair Labor Practice charges** at the National Labor Relations Board for threatening and discriminating against organizing janitors, numerous incidents of **disrespect** in the workplace (in some cases, reports of outright **racial prejudice**), and **unsafe working conditions** with OSHA workplace investigations.

To learn more and find out how you can support EMS janitors, log onto:

www.emsexposed.org

Service Employees International Union, 513.721.3096
This is not a request to cease services or deliveries

SEIU had also taken our fight to cyberspace with the introduction of a website called www.EMSexposed.org. One of the headlines, along with photographs of SEIU demonstrations, read, "How Cleaning Firm Executive Management Services is Hurting Hardworking Families in the Midwest" (claims that were fabricated and blatantly untrue). Ouch!

To add to the pressure being exerted on customers, during the middle of December, local clergy requested a meeting with officials of a state university we cleaned in Cincinnati. Simultaneously, protests were being held in that city and Indianapolis where strikers sang Christmas songs using protest-type language. And a new flyer appeared with the caption, "All We Want For Christmas" followed by a list, "EMS Janitors' Christmas List—End to Unfair Labor Practices, Respect, Justice." To accentuate their cause, Christmas baskets containing vinegar, rags, and gloves were left at the doorsteps of various building businesses, an apparent ploy to make those business owners feel guilty about the poor workers being treated like dirt by EMS. The truth is that vinegar is a terrific cleaning agent, we gave our workers plenty of rags, and the gloves were first-rate especially because we owned a supply company known for its first-class products. But I should not have worried as the business owners knew better, and so did the union. We treated the employees with respect and nearly 5,000 of them could testify to that if given the chance.

Those who say the Good Lord works in mysterious ways must have been referring to a blessing occurring on December 19, just six days before Christmas. All along I had wondered about the long list of clergy names (125 in all) attached to Rev. Cushman Wood's letters. I finally received my answer when Rev. Msgr. Joseph Schaedel, Vicar General and Moderator of the Curia (the Archbishop's right-hand man) wrote a letter to Rev. Hawking. And what a letter it was.

Rev. Schaedel began by explaining that although Rev. Hawking had asked the Archbishop and him to support the Interfaith Worker Justice cause on behalf of EMS employees and their right to organize, he had taken some time to investigate before making a decision. He told Rev. Hawking first that "Persons familiar with Catholic Social Teaching know that the Church supports the rights of workers, including workers' rights to organize into labor unions in order to negotiate with employers." He also admitted "It seems to me that our Catholic Social Teaching would support the principles espoused by Interfaith Worker Justice: It is our calling to keep before this city a vision of God's justice and mercy."

If these words heightened Rev. Hawking's view that Rev. Schaedel was about to endorse the IWJ's fight, she was dead wrong for the next paragraph began, "In good conscience, I <u>cannot</u> sign my name to this petition. In fairness, let me briefly tell you why." What followed were several bullet-point paragraphs explaining, among other matters: 1) there existed a conflict of interest as IWJ was "closely aligned" with SEIU, "a major financial contributor to IWJ;" 2) "rights of workers" meant letting workers decide for themselves whether they wanted to unionize after both the union and management presented "their respective case to the workers," a reference to this not occurring according to union demands; 3) that EMS had filed numerous charges against SEIU with the NLRB and after "talking to some of our Catholic immigrant workers who work at various other companies, I have reason to believe that these charges are true;" and 4) some workers have been told "by union organizers and members of IWJ that they will receive 12 dollars per hour as 'workers did in Cincinnati,'" but that "Catholic leaders in Cincinnati report that the union settled for just over seven dollars per hour, plus the employees had to pay 40 dollars a month for union dues. This would leave many I know (who presently make at least eight dollars per hour) worse off than they were before."

As a final bullet point, Rev. Schaedel suggested that based on his presence in downtown Indianapolis "over the past several months," and his receipt of flyers from "union organizers making various claims about various companies," he felt "even a surface investigation on my part reveals that most of those claims are simply false. Without <u>truth</u>, there will not be 'justice and mercy.'"

To emphasize his feelings, Rev. Schaedel added what I considered to be an important sentence, ". . . our Catholic clergy and other leaders must follow their own <u>informed</u> consciences in this regard." How I wished this would occur—where all of the clergy as well as those pointing fingers at EMS and me would take the time to learn the true facts.

Rev. Schaedel then wrote, ". . . as Vicar General, I want to make it clear that signatures of Catholic Clergy do not constitute a formal declaration of support for this initiative by the Catholic Archdiocese of Indianapolis. Nor does it necessarily constitute former support of the Catholic parishes in which they serve. In most cases, the majority of parishioners seem to have no idea that their pastor has even signed such a petition or joined the Indianapolis Clergy Committee."

In fact, Rev. Schaedel pointed out, "in talking to Catholic priests, whose names are listed, I find it worrisome that few of them seem to know what they were actually signing. In fact, at least one of the pastors whose name is listed has no idea how or why his name was included!"

To close the letter, the Vicar said that while he advocated fair wages and benefits, and that the workers be treated with dignity and respect, "I am not in agreement with the tactics currently being employed by Interfaith Worker Justice and the union to accomplish these goals."

Kissing a priest might cause some to blush during these times of political correctness, but if Rev. Schaedel had been present when I read his letter, I would have kissed him regardless of the consequences. Certainly, his letter made it clear to Rev. Hawking, Rev. Wood, and the others that SEIU was using clergy and employees solely for the union's own personal gain. SEIU didn't give a darn about such shenanigans in accordance with Stern's credo—using the persuasion of power to win at all cost.

On December 23, one pastor, Steven C. Schwab, reacted to Rev. Schaedel's letter by sending one of his own to Rev. Hawking. In part, it read, "I have learned that my name has been listed as a member of the Indianapolis Clergy Committee of Interfaith Worker Justice. At no time have I taken any action to associate myself with this group . . . I must insist that my name be at once removed from any association with this group."

As 2008 drifted into view, I still had hope that our "surge" initiative in filing the 33 charges against SEIU and letters such as the one sent by Rev. Schaedel might finally end the EMS–SEIU war. Certainly we had wounded the enemy, but it remained to be seen whether our strong stand had killed our foe. It hadn't, at least not yet.

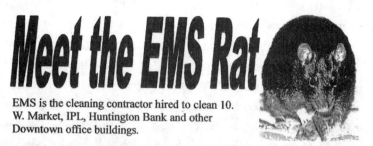

Meet the EMS Rat

EMS is the cleaning contractor hired to clean 10. W. Market, IPL, Huntington Bank and other Downtown office buildings.

Why is EMS a Rat Contractor?

Unfair Labor Practices:

The NLRB has issued a complaint on 8 counts against EMS for illegal, surveillance, threats of job loss, interrogation, and retaliation against workers engaged in legally protected activity.
EMS is facing additional charges for illegally firing, coercing, and restraining employees engaged in protected activity.

Unsafe working conditions:

IOSHA has found violations of IOSHA safety standards by EMS at Market Tower including:
Damaged Electrical Extension Cord
Unlabeled Bottles of Hazardous Chemicals

EMS Janitors at Market Tower are on an Unfair Labor Practice Strike. 1/9/08

Dispute with EMS and no other Employer.

On a cold and windy January 11, two days after a U-Haul truck with a rat in it was paraded before Market Tower, IFW held a prayer meeting. On Martin Luther King Day, January 21, SEIU sponsored a "Pray for Justice, March for Working Families" event. The union was not about to give up as the war extended beyond the two-year mark as evidenced by a new flyer being circulated featuring the words, "Corporations in Indianapolis Generate $1 Billion A Day; Janitors who clean their offices and laboratories earn as little as $26 a day without affordable health insurance. Something Is Wrong Here."

Attempting to satisfy his EMS contract commitments, his investors, and placate SEIU, Gerald Donaldson decided to "remain neutral" in the dispute. In a late January letter, he informed Revs. Woods and Hawking his company "would support any process that can be agreed upon between the two parties as an effective mechanism for determining whether or not employees wish to be represented by SEIU." To indicate his support for workers, the company agreed to a "matching challenge of up to 25,000 dollars or to establish a scholarship fund for the City's janitors in coordination with the Islamic Society of North America and Interfaith Worker Justice." Reading the letter made me wonder what Revs. Woods and Hawking, and of course, SEIU, thought of my customers' position. I was certainly pleased that Gerald was sticking by us and more than willing to agree to an acceptable process toward deciding whether EMS employees wanted to be unionized. Because the law provided for the secret-ballot elections, all we had to do was follow the law.

It appears the responses from Gerald and Reverend Schaedel were not what the union expected and escalated the attacks against EMS. Beside a large photograph of a rat were the words, "Meet The EMS Rat" followed by "Why is EMS a Rat Contractor?" and "Unfair Labor Practices . . . Unsafe Working Conditions." Under this were the words, "Damaged Electrical Extension Cord, Unlabeled Bottles of Hazardous Chemicals."

Reading this flyer made me want to take the afternoon off from the world. Imagine how badly I felt and then triple those feelings. For the company I had founded and loved to be labeled with such words as "rat" was simply beyond comprehension. And yes, while the electrical cord and unlabeled bottles were technically violations, they were miniscule in stature. But it didn't matter, the union was going to use these violations to show how evil we were, how we didn't care about safe employee working conditions. Ah, the power of words, the ability to choose what to say and what not to say so the worst surfaced for those who knew no better. If I thought the war was over, I was sadly mistaken. We had simply entered another phase of the costly encounter.

To further the quest to embarrass EMS, four people, one dressed in a gray rat costume, appeared at an appreciation luncheon sponsored by IFMA for contractors like EMS on January 25. Even though the meeting was by invitation only and held in a private room at a local establishment, SEIU organizers violated private property and pushed pass the hostess into the room where they handed out yellow flyers. They only left when officials threatened to call the police.

Through February, March, and April, less union activity occurred causing me to hope the worst might be over. Also, during this time period the union was in contract negotiations with contractors that had signed Neutrality Agreements. I was anxious to see the final contract as I anticipated it would be subpar just as the ones in Houston and most recently Cincinnati had been. It would be an opportunity to prove the only benefit the union was providing was the questionable right for the employees to pay union dues. Additionally, we expected soon a decision on the charges EMS had filed against the union for illegal recognitional picketing and secondary boycotting. We were not disappointed in the outcome of either situation and it appeared our efforts were beginning to bear fruit.

The contract, despite a press release by the SEIU touting a great victory for janitors, was anything but that and, in reality, a step back. Starting wages were set at seven dollars per hour less 25 cents per hour for the probation period at a time when the majority of janitors were starting at that or higher in Indianapolis. It also had a provision for an increase of 30 cents per hour for existing employees that barely covered monthly union dues. The union's boast of up to 150 percent increase in wages was based on the same claims made in Cincinnati, already mentioned except for one major point. Every SEIU contract I have seen has a provision where building owners can set the hours based on security or energy demands. Basically this results in no change of operational hours in those buildings and as a result little or no increase in full-time employment. Additionally, they touted the fact that janitors now had recourse from management harassment and abuse.

Digressing some, in discussions with union companies in both Cincinnati and Indianapolis because contracts have been negotiated and ratified in both cities, I have consistently heard the SEIU is disorganized and does not monitor any provisions of the contract very well including wages, benefits, hours of work, and worker rights. Basically, it's business as usual for the contractors, and the SEIU keeps collecting monthly dues from the employees. Maybe this explains why so many companies sign the Neutrality Agreements, something my sense of right and wrong would not allow me to do to my employees!

In April 2008, the Indianapolis regional office of the NLRB issued a complaint against the SEIU on the basis of charges we had filed in 2007. The complaint alleged that the union had engaged in illegal secondary boycotting at a local area golf course, as well as in illegal recognitional picketing at numerous downtown Indianapolis locations where EMS employees worked. This was a major victory for EMS, as we had demonstrated that the union's months of picketing activities and related protests had extended beyond the permissible 30-day period with the union having requested an NLRB election.

These series of events set the stage for the SEIU to sign an agreement with the NLRB that they would not picket EMS or conduct a secondary boycott of EMS in central Indiana. The union was told that if they did not agree to discontinue their illegal picketing activities, the NLRB was prepared to go to federal court to seek an injunction preventing them from doing do. With the writing on the wall, the union agreed to stop violating the law in this way.

At that point the NLRB put pressure on me to sign an agreement settling a series of unfair labor practices that the union had filed alleging we had threatened or coerced EMS employees. I knew the allegations were blatantly false and simply a part of the union's arsenal of words against me, but in hopes that these settlements would bring an end to the war, I agreed to post a notice saying that EMS would not violate the law—already true before we posted the notice. In settling these charges, EMS did not admit any liability or wrongdoing.

All of this set the stage for the next major battle, strikers' reinstatement, an important part of the SEIU's Corporate Campaign playbook, which I did not fully understand at the time even though I suspected it was a major plank in their campaign.

In May, we received a new challenge—several of the striking EMS workers asked to be reinstated. While I sympathized with their plight and truly believed they had been used by SEIU based on exaggerated claims as to what the union could do for them, we had to stand firm with our convictions that the strike was an economic strike and not an unfair labor practice strike, and that the strikers engaged in illegal recognitional picketing which the union had been found guilty of by the NLRB. I also had compassion for the replacements who had the courage to defy the union by accepting employment during a difficult time. I had great respect for these people and was not about to turn my back on them when they had been there for me.

Through May, June, and July, the union pressed on. Several people accosted Dee, an EMS employee, as she left work at 11:00 p.m. Despite her telling them she was not interested, they harassed her as she walked away. Writing about this is easy to do, but it is important to remember how Dee, a quiet woman just trying to make money for her family, must have felt alone late at night as the workers approached her. I am sure she was scared; the exact feeling the union expected and wanted to occur. All because people like Dee had no taste for SEIU and their ruthless campaign to force unionization on hard working employees regardless of the consequences. Following the sorry episode, Dee wrote a letter to EMS expressing her appreciation for EMS's support."

Letters to customers, including one from Rev. Woods to the Market Tower building owner "urging them to choose a different [cleaning] contractor" continued in July. Drum-banging and foghorn-yelling also continued as union supporters yelled, "EMS Has To Go." On September 23, Allison Luthie, Community Organizer for Jobs With Justice sent a scathing letter to the Tenants at "101 W Ohio." The lengthy first sentence read, "As you may know, seventeen individuals who work in the building in which your office is located are about to lose their jobs because your landlord, Amerimar Enterprises, has chosen to end its contract with their employer and begin a new contract with another cleaning company whose record as an employer leaves much to be desired." She further explained that the reference was to janitors who had "helped make history" by "organizing as part of the Indianapolis Justice for Janitors campaign." Having set her agenda, Allison then attacked EMS writing, "During the past several years we have heard many negative reports about EMS and its labor relations practice that suppress the rights of workers and perpetuate poverty in our community . . . . We found the stories of several current and former EMS workers from Indianapolis and Cincinnati, Ohio to be deeply disturbing. They told us of being subjected to a hostile work environment that includes unsafe working conditions and racial discrimination."

Replacing a union contractor as the cleaning source for this building had obviously struck a chord with Luthie, which was not surprising since the SEIU was a dues paying member of Jobs With Justice. But stating that we perpetuated poverty in the community and were guilty of racial discrimination was totally out of bounds and a true distortion of the facts! Regardless of these facts, Luthie had defamed our company. Lawsuits could be filed against Jobs With Justice just as they could have been filed against SEIU for any number of defamatory remarks and actions. But this was not my way. Certainly, I had hired legal counsel to defend our rights before the NLRB, and certainly I consulted with the attorneys regarding many of our actions, but I did not want to sue anyone unless absolutely necessary. But the temptation was there to haul JWJ into court, an organization totally in SEIU's pocket despite their website motto, "building a strong, progressive labor movement that works in coalition with community, faith, and student organizations to build a broader global movement for economic and social justice." Basically, JWJ was an extension of the SEIU, one that believed "organizing and mobilizing working people and their allies is key to building power." One specific goal of theirs was: "Develop leaders and activists to lead our fights," something quite evident during the SEIU campaign to destroy EMS.

Many JWJ organizers had participated in song and prayer rallies in August when flyers were being passed out and cowbells used to bring attention to worker demonstrations. During late September, EMS employees at the university reported that SEIU organizers were outside the college chanting, "Hi, Ho, Hi, Ho, EMS Has Got To Go." On October 1, tension nearly produced violence again when an employee of an EMS customer blocked a door where SEIU organizers and Interfaith Clergy were trying to enter. The employee was pushed causing her to spill coffee on one of the Clergy members. Police were called before any fights broke out. The clergy member filed a police complaint but later withdrew it.

Five days later, SEIU tried another tactic, one causing me to throw my arms up in disbelief. Outside one of our buildings in downtown Indianapolis, about a dozen bags of trash were left on the sidewalk. Flyers stated that "Amerimar Treats Janitors Like Trash," a reference to our customer. All I could do was apologize to those folks and tell them I hoped that such childish actions would cease soon and once and for all. But the incidents did not stop because in mid-November, union organizers collected in front of Amerimar's Philadelphia headquarters where they protested and handed out flyers. A month later in Cincinnati, SEIU representatives chanted and passed out flyers outside the Hixson Building. One union organizer blocked a door so employees could not enter. Police were finally called to quench any possible violence.

Victory

Despite hopes SEIU would disappear into the sunset, the year 2009 brought more conflict with the union. And continued heated debate about the controversial Employee Free Choice Act as union leaders like Stern pushed politicians toward a vote in the Senate. I proceeded along two fronts, continuing to fend off attempts by SEIU to destroy my company and a separate campaign to reveal the truth about the un-American nature of the EFCA, a threat to life, liberty, and the pursuit of happiness, if there ever was one.

On the SEIU side, we noted several attempts during the early months to continue the dirty campaign against EMS, but of main concern were the upcoming NLRB hearings. I knew we were the underdog going in based on our interaction with the Board to that point.

The rub centered on EMS's refusal to reinstate strikers who asked to be brought back to work when the strike ended. Remember in May 2008, the union had agreed not to picket or secondary boycott EMS. In exchange, we agreed to settle 13 outstanding NLRB complaints. This appeared to be a good deal on both ends, with my hope the SEIU would drift away and leave our employees, customers, company, and me alone.

In life, many times we get hoodwinked when we are so intent on agreeing to something that later on we know was too good to be true. But we decide doing so makes good common sense especially when we are tired of fighting the fight and just want some peace. This was my mindset when the agreement was reached for EMS to settle the 13 complaints, minor as they were. By doing so, I hoped to put the SEIU mess behind me and move forward. I thus forgot to watch my backside, a mistake that would cost me dearly, both personally and business-wise.

The allegations against EMS dating from January 2007 included a variety of charges, each of which could have been defended to our satisfaction. But the carrot tempting me to agree to a "non-admission of guilt" document, a "Notice to Employees" that would be posted in customer buildings for 60 days, was the union's agreement that no more picketing and no more customer inference would occur. When NLRB officials contacted us and proposed, actually pushed this resolution, we felt we needed to listen.

When I looked at the specifics of the notice, my reaction was to believe that all we were doing was agreeing to what the law required, what we had been doing all along, and nothing more. Among the provisions was the statement: "Federal Law Gives You The Right To: Form, Join, or Assist a union; Choose representation to bargain with us on your behalf; Act Together with other employees for your benefit and protection, and Choose not to engage in any of these activities." What would be wrong with those statements, I wondered. I believed in these rights to a T.

Listed under these words were the following: "We will not threaten you with job loss, discipline, discharge or other unspecified retaliation because you engage in activities on behalf of the SEIU, Local 3, or any other labor organization, because you talk about your terms and conditions of employment with other people outside the company, or because you engage in a lawful strike." Further, we agreed: "We will not ask you about your union activities. . . ., We will not watch your union activity . . . or threaten your union

The Devil at My Doorstep / David Bego

activity . . . We will not instruct you to remove your union buttons, and we will not prohibit you from wearing union buttons; We will not instruct you to not talk about the union or not to talk with a union representative; We will not delay issuing you your paycheck because you engage in union activities, including participating in a lawful strike, and We will not in any like or related manner interfere with, restrain, or coerce, you in the exercise of the rights guaranteed you by Section 7 of the act."

Once again, when I read these provisions, I knew we would, in essence, be agreeing to exactly what we had been doing all along. Additionally, there was a non-admission of liability statement absolving EMS of any wrongdoing. No change was necessary and I believed this was how a company should operate. How could I not sign an agreement stating these principles, especially if the SEIU was promising to end the war once and for all by waving the surrender flag.

Was I ready to get back to running the business on a daily basis? Certainly so, but this is no excuse as I knew what I was doing. Perhaps I was just tired of spending more money on legal fees and other costs as the total headed toward seven figures, or just wanted to give my employees and our customers a rest. Maybe I just thought this was the right thing to do, to give in a bit so I could once and for all say goodbye to Stern and his union. Regardless, I signed and every day I knew the notice of our agreeing never to do any of these things again was posted for all to see. This was fine with me because we never violated any of the laws. Additionally, we never heard one comment from employees about the postings. Had I made a mistake; maybe, but I always knew there was the possibility of the strikers asking for reinstatement and was content with that possibility. What I had not anticipated was the duplicity of the NLRB in processing these charges. Was I surprised at the NLRB's reversal and support of the SEIU's position?

Yes, I was, because a trap had been laid and I had fallen into it. Shortly after the agreement was reached, the union, on behalf of the employees, sent notices on behalf of eight of the strikers requesting reinstatement to work. Immediately I conferred with our attorneys and decided we were not going to honor the reinstatements for two reasons: first, and most importantly the NLRB had concluded that the union had engaged in illegal recognitional picketing activities and each of the strikers had personally participated in that illegal picketing, and second the strike was not as the union had alleged—an unfair labor practice strike. Past case law indicated that any striker participating in illegal recognitional picketing forfeited his or her rights to reinstatement.

The SEIU immediately filed NLRB charges stating that EMS wrongfully refused reinstatement to the strikers, because it was supposedly an unfair labor practice strike. We were very comfortable with our position, because we based it on the fact that the we had settled the frivolous unfair labor practices with no admission of guilt, and the union had agreed to end its illegal recognitional picketing. We were absolutely shocked when the NLRB in their infinite wisdom agreed with the union and decided to issue a complaint against EMS for failing to reinstate the strikers. Now I was not only continuing to fight the union, but also my own government. The NLRB offered to settle the charges if EMS agreed to reinstate the strikers with back pay, but I could not accept their proposal.

Early in 2009, we received notice that the NLRB hearing would be held in April debating our refusal to permit striking employees to return to work. Apparently knowing they had the NLRB in their back pocket, the SEIU had outwitted me and set us up so that now they could waltz EMS in front of the NLRB and make us defend our decision not to rehire the workers. I should have seen this coming, but my tactical error was apparent especially when we learned of the miniscule amount of evidence SEIU had regarding the 13 charges we had settled back in May of 2008. We would have wiped them up at a hearing, but instead settled. And when we did so, the union then directed the employees back to work, resulting in EMS declining their request.

Left on the table was thus the plight of ten (the NLRB decided to include the two strikers the union forgot to send EMS reinstatement letters to) employees who alleged EMS had not permitted them to return to their jobs after the strike. It was no surprise that the SEIU characterized the walkout as an unfair labor strike while we believed the strike was nothing more than an economic strike. To bolster their claim, a clever move, the union brought up the 13 charges we believed were now off the table due to the settlement. They were thrown in our face as a show of unfair treatment to the employees.

The SEIU's mischaracterization of the strike as an unfair labor practice strike was significant. If, as we believed, the union's unfair labor practice charges were merely a ruse and the union was striking for recognition, then the strikers would be ineligible for reinstatement. If on the other hand, EMS really had committed unfair labor practices and those were truly a reason for the strike, then workers may have been eligible for reinstatement. Even then, we believed that the union's illegal recognitional picketing that had continued for at least eight months was sufficiently severe so that the strikers had lost their right to reinstatement.

After the brief respite of inactivity during the first few months of 2009, the war resumed when the NLRB conducted the hearings in April. NLRB and SEIU attorneys began by presenting several witnesses to the administrative law judge all in an attempt to prove that the strike was based on alleged unfair labor practices by the company. But huge discrepancies soon appeared as our crack legal team cross-examined complaining employees when their stories conflicted with documented evidence we presented, and even their own previous sworn testimony. In numerous instances the strikers' testimony often supported EMS's claims that the strike was for recognition reasons and not unfair labor practice, and disputed supposed incidents of harassment by EMS managers and supervisors. Once again, our ability to chronicle every single incident occurring before and during the strike along with fresh information about the disgruntled employees the union convinced to strike made the difference. When the union had completed its side of the story through employee testimony, I spent two hours on the witness stand explaining our side of the story.

As I spoke, I could not help but temper my remarks about the employees because I knew they had been provided with false information and had been used by the union for its own purposes. But I had to tell the truth under oath and I did so by detailing the work-related problems we had with these employees including poor attendance, poor work performance, and in some cases, theft and incidences of threatening behavior against supervisors. I think the judge was impressed at how well we had documented each employee's track record and sensed his belief that the walk-out was anything but an unfair labor practices strike. Our legal team had the same impression to the extent that we believed through the judge's words that the union had indeed engaged in illegal recognitional picketing. This occurs when the union continues to picket after 30 days without petitioning for a secret-ballot election, a violation of the NLRA. In our case, the SEIU had not only repeatedly ignored our request for a secret-ballot election, but had openly told us they did not want an election, supposedly because it took too long.

On the topic of documentation and training, one thing we learned along the way is that the SEIU has no formalized training programs or manuals. Why? Much like what we have learned about ACORN (under investigation for voter fraud and, as mentioned, a close ally of the SEIU), they do not want any documentation that could convict them if they are investigated for working outside of the law. They also do not want any smoking guns that can be traced back to the corporate headquarters. I have always found that outstanding corporations, businesses that have nothing to hide, document and train to a fault. Our discovery concerning the SEIU did not surprise me at all!

Witnesses we called substantiated these claims. Every one of the strikers seeking reinstatement admittedly had been engaged in picketing EMS during the eight-month strike. Just as importantly, EMS was able to credibly refute all of the supposed unfair labor practice claims that the SEIU was using to establish the strike as an unfair labor practice strike. When the hearings concluded, I was hopeful the judge would rule in our favor. Clearly the evidence had substantiated our position, but many times before we felt this way, only to be broadsided by a ruling against us. This was especially true regarding the incident where the large banner was draped over the side of a customer's building in Cincinnati. No real question existed that SEIU was responsible, but the NLRB sided with them because of a lack of proof the union was behind the action. The NLRB said we had no physical documentation that the people were union organizers or supporters, despite the fact that one of our employees had witnessed the event and two days later union organizers were on the corner passing out photographs of the banner and a flyer defaming EMS. Hard to believe, but true. Does common sense not count for anything? Additionally the NLRB was now backing off their earlier ruling that the SEIU had participated in illegal recognitional picketing, even though they had signed an agreement with the SEIU preventing then from doing so! What?

Such rulings were proof positive, to my way of thinking, of the bias of the NLRB against business and management. While the labor board was supposed to be objective, time and time again we experienced a feeling that we were presumed to be guilty and had to fight to prove our innocence. The NLRB siding with the SEIU provided the SEIU the confidence that their best shot at beating us was certainly before the board and not in a court of law. This is why union leaders like Stern insist on binding arbitration as a pivotal element of the Employee Free Choice Act legislation. If it passes, businesses like mine are doomed because no legal recourse is possible if we disagree with union negotiation regarding contracts. All the union has to do is to make absurd demands, ones surely rejected, and then head toward arbitration presided over by government-appointed officials. A government with a lot of politicians indebted to unions because of election wins (in private elections, I might add) based on massive union campaign donations. In fact current rumor is that Stern has a weekly meeting with President Obama. This is not justice in any form, Stern and the SEIU don't care.

On June 23, 2009, rays of sunshine broke through on what was otherwise a dreary day. Our attorney informed us that EMS had been exonerated of the charges filed by the SEIU that it had unlawfully failed to reinstate the striking employees. In a sweeping decision, the Administrative Law Judge for the NLRB found that the SEIU had failed to prove the vast majority of the alleged unfair labor practices by EMS and that, in any event, the alleged unfair labor practices were not a motivating cause for the strike. The judge also ruled that EMS did not have to reinstate 10 former strikers, because they had engaged in illegal recognitional picketing in violation of Section 8(b)(7)(C) of the National Labor Relations Act. The judge was very clear that the testimony provided by the SEIU witnesses was contrived, contradictory and not believable. He stated for example, "These witnesses are not credible because when testifying they appeared to be more interested in supporting a litigation theory than in testifying candidly." Wow, the judge got it right! What a great victory for not only EMS and its employees, but for companies and employees across the country who are willing to stand up to the bully tactics of unions like the SEIU!

Eight days later, however, I sat in my office not in disbelief, but rather with disillusionment and concern for where our great country is headed. I had just received a call from our attorney, Greg Guevara, who had spoken to legal counsel from the regional NLRB office in Indiana. Mike Beck, the NLRB attorney, informed Greg that the General Counsel for the Washington NLRB had directly instructed him to appeal the case to the National Board. This seemed incredulous at first since an NLRB Administrative Law Judge had made the ruling which was, beyond a shadow of a doubt, the correct decision! However, I knew the striker reinstatement decision in our favor had been a severe blow to the SEIU. It effectively eliminated one of the major planks in their Corporate Campaign to bully companies into signing a neutrality or recognition agreement, thus substituting card check in place of a secret ballot election. I also suspected they would call in political markers to have the decision overturned. Why? Because pressuring a company's employees into striking and engaging in recognitional picketing is the SEIU's last-ditch effort in its Corporate Campaign to embarrass and intimidate an employer into signing a recognition agreement. It fact, this was openly expressed during testimony by one of the SEIU's witnesses during the hearing. It was obvious in his brief, the judge clearly understood that the unfair labor practices, the strike and the picketing had been manufactured for one purpose, to pressure EMS into signing a Neutrality Agreement, nevertheless the NLRB was set to appeal. Although not surprised by the turn of events, my blood pressure was rising once again!

Despite our attorney's belief that an appeal by the NLRB on the union's behalf made no sense, it was not unexpected and very clear to me. In my mind (and I am not a conspiracy theory believer) Stern and the SEIU were introducing their proclaimed "persuasion of power" via their association with the White House. I believe that the SEIU contacted the Obama administration when they learned of the decision, who in turn made a call to the General Council of the NLRB in Washington D.C. and demanded an appeal of the case. (Again, it is widely reported that Stern has a weekly meeting with President Obama.) Despite an overwhelming decision in EMS's favor, the SEIU is betting on its political influence to have the case overturned. Classic SEIU "persuasion of power" is based on political contributions and ideology, but in my mind it is political corruption. It is a shame that Stern and the SEIU, who could not even win on a playing field tilted in their favor, now have to resort to using political pressure to achieve their objectives.

Earlier in the book, I mentioned that Stern was apparently unsuccessful in the private sector, but became so in the union environment where he could use his bully tactics. This latest development reinforces my suspicions, and even sadder, it appears the current administration of our country may be complicit in the "persuasion of power." How terrifying for the future of all of us!

Despite the latest developments, I am optimistic that our system of government will continue to vindicate EMS, but we the people must continue to be vigilant and remove politicians on both sides of the aisle who abuse their positions and power. Even with the probability of surviving the war with Stern and the SEIU, a multi-headed monster lurks in the future—the Employee Free Choice Act (EFCA). But as it makes its way to the Senate floor where passage remains unclear, I am more concerned with presenting a plan whereby unions will leave a company like mine alone through the realization that 1) we treat our employees with dignity and respect, paying them the highest wages in the industry along with good benefits, while still remaining competitive in the marketplace; and 2) we are willing, according to the law, to permit secret-ballot elections at any point in time if our employees want to consider unionization.

This reasonable, common-sense attitude is based on a strong employer–employee foundation built, more than anything else, on one important factor—trust. During my 20-plus years of owning and operating my own business, lessons learned along the way helped me build this trust. The result is a number of tips that might help others who want to start their own business, grow it, and then sustain it using solid business practices with the main focus on how to treat fairly the front-line employees who bust their butts every day to make the company successful so everyone wins in the end. If the company does this, then a union is not needed to protect those workers.

Before anyone decides to start their own business, several factors must be weaved into the equation; owning and running your own business is not for everyone. People have to ask themselves whether they are willing to take the risk, to give up the security of working for others who take the risk. One important question to ask—whether there is enough inner strength to start from nothing with an unsure future—doing so is not for the faint of heart.

Another consideration—there is no eight to five workday schedule possible when you own your own business. Good ideas are commonplace, and while a good idea is the bud for starting a business, too often people don't have the discipline and work ethic to work their tails off especially during the initial stages when it is make it or break it time. Stating it another way, when you own your own business, there is no quitting time as the business has to come first 24 hours a day seven days a week. Focus and direction are key too, and persistence, a trait I learned from competitive sports and from my parents. You have to decide to try, and then try and try again and never give up, or give in.

While I doubt they would admit it, my bet is the SEIU learned this about me when I wouldn't cave in to its demands. Call it dumb, call it stupid, especially when the odds favor your opposition, whether it is a person, a union, or another obstacle, but "persistence," the quality of continually moving forward in the face of adversity, is a trait all those who operate there own business must have, especially when someone or some entity is trying to destroy the business. There is no throwing in your hand when you take on the world single-handedly. Through good times and bad, a business owner must suck it up and keep going even when others want them to fail. Some days it will feel like the weight of the world is on your shoulders, and you can't go on, but you have to. There is no choice in the matter because your savings, or bank financing, or financing provided by love ones, colleagues or investors, is at stake—no running out the back door is permitted but instead hard work, and then more hard work. This type of mindset is the only thing that permitted me to have a chance when Stern and the SEIU wanted to crush me. I simply told myself nobody was going to take my freedom away from me, my share of the American Dream. Nobody.

Another key element to starting a business is enough capital. Most businesses fail because of this when poor financial planning causes shortcuts, even though an all-out effort is required. Revenues are going to be sparse for the first few months, or even years, until some sort of a profit and cash flow may be realized. Keeping the business going during these times with enough money to pay the bills and pay yourself so you can feed your family is essential so there is no worry about where the next nickel or dime is coming from. Making a profit is one thing, but cash flow is king—a concept many do not understand.

Any smart person deciding to start his or her own business tries like hell to take on as little debt as possible. When Barb and I began EMS, we used our own personal savings to finance the company and thus avoided borrowing money we would have to pay back eventually. To this day, our company has run daily operations off cash flow and not borrowed funds providing flexibility and independence when otherwise we would have been paying a bank or another financial institution that might want to dictate how we run our business. Just imagine if we had been heavily in debt when the SEIU war began. Then the financial institution would have been looking over our shoulder worried that our reputation was being tarnished. But because we are fiscally conservative, we could charge ahead and do what we knew was right—defend our employees against unwanted or unsolicited pressure and harassment.

Speaking of money, one pitfall for business owners is allegiance to the almighty dollar. In today's world, unfortunately, too much emphasis is put on becoming rich and famous. Look at all the unhappy people who have millions or even billions of dollars, more money than they could ever spend in 10 lifetimes, and yet they have very little peace of mind. So while profit is important, the question remains how much profit is reasonable, especially if those working to help you make a profit are being treated unfairly. Maybe I am thickheaded, but it doesn't make any sense at all to me to treat employees with disrespect or try to keep them at poverty level when they are the real key to success. This is why allegations by the SEIU made me sick when they said EMS paid "poverty wages." Nothing could have been further from the truth and the union knew it.

The real key, money-wise, to running a successful self-owned business is cash flow. Meeting payroll is essential to earning employee respect, and good cash flow and a reasonable profit permit one to meet employee needs, and think of acquisitions and capital investment. Bad cash flow is a killer; an absolute killer dooming many start-ups to failure. But good cash flow opens up many opportunities for growth and for times when money is needed for emergency purposes. If EMS had not had sufficient cash flow, where would the money have come from to fight SEIU? How blessed we were that we could hire expert attorneys and pay them without going deeply in debt.

Relationships are what owning your own business is all about. From day one, I preached this to our sales and operations people, and to those who cleaned the buildings and plants. Our customers are the real bosses and we work for them, not the other way around. There is thus the need to listen to their concerns, and listen again, and then attempt to fulfill their needs every day on a quality basis with a sense of urgency. That's how a good reputation is born, and how relationships like many EMS enjoys have lasted for decades. Loyalty from those customers becomes unquestioned even when attempts to soil a reputation are undertaken. I get teary-eyed when I think of people like Gerald who's wife had to put up with the SEIU trick or treaters , and other valued

EMS customers who stuck by us when SEIU was assaulting the company at every turn. Without them, EMS would have been devastated.

Relationships with "good-hearted" customers are essential to the growth of any self-owned business. Why work with bad people even though a good profit might be possible? In the long run, these bad people will prove to be a source of irritation, especially since you can't trust them. I can't count how many times EMS passed up substantial business, or canceled contracts, when we realized those we were doing business with were not ones we wanted to do business with.

Servicing good customers means servicing them every hour of every day. Becoming complacent is the enemy of any business and a death knell for self-owned businesses that rely on fewer customers than the big boys. Show you care, every day, and in every way. It's like the waiter or waitress who keeps coming back to fill your coffee cup or check to see if your food is okay. Little things mean a lot in the business world and customers appreciate a telephone call or a letter checking to see if the service you are providing is up to speed.

Hiring good, solid, hard-working, honest, and ethical employees is essential to any successful business. Fortunately, I found four or five of those in my family, a true blessing if ever there was one. They cared about EMS as much as I did, and we planned together and worked together to build a business of which we all can be proud. And they, along with other long-term top management, were there for me when we fought Stern and the SEIU. Without a hitch, our business kept going without me contributing as much as I normally would have done. Perhaps they enjoyed my being away so much, or at least my mind being away so I wouldn't bother them. I'm afraid to ask.

As for the front-line employees, selecting those who have the same value systems regarding hard work is key. "You are your employees" is a nice slogan to consider because those people wearing the EMS logo on their shirts represent the company every day. If they are trustworthy, honest, and hardworking, customers know this and appreciate it. But if they are not, customers notice this as well. There are many examples where EMS, despite not having the lowest bid, won a nice contract based on our employee reputations. Compensate and treat employees well and they will treat you well and with respect—the core of any relationship. Additionally, with the threat of EFCA hanging over everyone's head, training for managers, supervisors, and hourly employees concerning EFCA and union organizational tactics is a good idea. EMS has developed and copyrighted simple training pamphlets that use pictures to help get the message across in a manner that captures interest, understanding, and retention.

In addition to providing good working environments where employees don't have to be concerned about safety, it is important to make certain workers feel free to express dissatisfaction with any number of areas of concern. At union plants I managed, I learned that the inability to express dissatisfaction is a major employee irritation whether complaints focus on working conditions, work products, or personal issues. The latter are especially important to EMS, because we never want any employee to be scared to report for work or feel threatened while at work. When the company was a year- or two-old, a young, African-American woman told me, "Mr. Bego, I'm being sexually harassed by the supervisor in my building." Because she was 20 and the supervisor was in his late 70s (what does age have to do with anyone's ability to do a job well?), I immediately investigated. The older fellow had gone through some tough times to the extent that I loaned him some cash to get by. I talked to him and discovered that he and the young woman had been romantically involved despite their age difference. But he had fallen deeply in love with her and didn't want the relationship to end. We moved the woman into another building after I warned him to stay away from her. He understood and we never had any problems after that.

Sometimes employees just need someone to talk to or to listen to their problems. Through the years I've heard more confessions than most priests but I feel honored employees trust me enough to share their deepest concerns. And they know I keep what they tell me confidential because I respect their privacy. We're all human, we all make mistakes, and we all need people to rely on when times are tough.

Back to starting the business, you must have a vision of what you want to do and how it is a different from the ones that exist already in the industry. Possessing what I call "good business sense" is important, as is understanding the marketplace, and how your product or service might compete. Good business sense allows for development of a sound game plan when the time arrives to grow your business. Determination and the will to survive carry one only so far until more risk is necessary when growth opportunities present themselves. While we were pleased with EMS company expansion in Indiana, we decided to grow into other areas of the Midwest and beyond. With integrity and good camaraderie with our employees as a staple, we took the leap and moved EMS from a small, local company to a company that could compete successfully with the largest companies in our industry. Our EMS team—management, clerical, the front-line employees, expert lawyers, and accountants—propelled us to a position of respect in the cleaning maintenance business. That's why Stern and the SEIU faced such stiff competition when they decided to wage war.

Politics

ON FEBRUARY 4, 2009, I HAD THE PLEASURE OF APPEARING ON CNN'S *Lou Dobbs Show* to discuss the SEIU and the Employee Free Choice Act. Investigative reporter Drew Griffin had actually prerecorded the interview a week earlier at my office.

In the segment, I was able to provide EMS's side of the story and felt I did so in a fair manner. Conversely, Stern was also interviewed for the segment and came across as dictatorial and threatening in accordance with how he runs the SEIU. In fact, he made two comments directly to the politicians he helped get elected. First, all politicians better keep their promises or else, and second, everybody should be scared about failing to live up to their promises. Wow—can you imagine the everyday person, or business owners, threatening the politicians and our President in this manner? They would be crucified in the media and publicly. I cannot imagine people wanting to be part of an organization run by such an individual. (Go to http://www.youtube.com/watch?v=ru5D4u2Q4QY.)

To further my ideas about the SEIU and the EFCA, I sent a five-page letter on March 4, 2009 to every member of Congress, House of Representatives and Senate alike, regarding the Employee Free Choice Act. I received less than 20 responses in return. What puzzles me is that few people seem to be listening. Deaf ears are the call of the day and I truly believe there are two main reasons why this is occurring. First, the very nature of the name of the pending legislation is attractive. Who wants to vote against something with the words "Free Choice?" Second, the political process, and the SEIU's ability to influence politicians exists to the extent they would vote for any legislation the union supports. Millions of dollars in donations permit labor to carry a big stick and those politicians accepting the money know they better step up in favor of union legislation or, as Stern, has vowed, be targeted come election time. Cross the unions, the SEIU in particular, and the comfy job with all the benefits and nice salary in Washington disappears with the loser relegated to a "real job" back in their home state.

In my letter, I tried like blazes to open some eyes. I established my credential as a business owner of some length before writing, "Today I write to ask for your support in stopping a bill that I believe will cripple almost every business and industry in this country." Based on that sentence alone, I would have expected the telephone to start ringing and a hundred e-mails to pour through my inbox. But nothing like this occurred. Perhaps it was because I'm from Indianapolis, far away from either coast where the real important people in the country live, or so many believe. Or maybe the fact that I operate a cleaning business didn't quite register with those who care more about a company like GM on the brink of bankruptcy. Whatever the reason—almost dead silence was the result except for the small percentage of responses heard.

If the above sentence didn't gain much attention, I had hoped the first two in paragraph four would. They read, "The so-called 'Employee Free Choice Act,' an ineptly named bill supported by organized labor (but not the vast majority of business owners or employees), is not really about employee 'free choice.' In truth, this legislation is about taking away the individual employee's freedom to choose whether they want to join a union or not—in an atmosphere free from intimidation and coercion."

The next four pages laid out my concerns about the act. I gave the politicians every reason I could think of triggering my belief that the EFCA was a dangerous piece of legislation. I detailed the vigorous, ruthless campaign against EMS and how the union "employs the exact practices of intimidation, harassment, lies, coercion, bribes and threats it accuses the company of in its propaganda." The result of such tactics, I explained, "is that unions are not only mistrusted by the company, but more importantly, by the exact audience they target—the company's employees." Bidding to make my case that readers consider the impact of the legislation, I ended the letter with the following: "Please remember that you were chosen for your public service by a secret-ballot election. The core value of freedom of choice, in a secret process free from coercion and outside pressure, is central to our democracy. Are you willing to enact a law that would take away the fundamental freedom from American workers? If not, I urge you to oppose the Employees Free Choice Act," with the final two sentences in bold so as to emphasize their importance. This especially rings true with today's current events in Iran where people are dying to obtain a true secret ballot process that is not corrupt. Most members of Congress and our President are pressuring Iran to allow a true and uncorrupt secret ballot election process. Yet they are preparing to do just the opposite in the United States of America (the most free country in the world) by passing the Employee Free Choice Act and eliminating an individual's right to a secret ballot election in the work place.

During the days when my letter was forwarded, EFCA was in the news, with a *CNN* article reporting: "Key Union Renews Push For Hotly Contested Labor Bill." Included in the fourth paragraph was a statement by Stern: "[Business leaders] believe in this old market-worshipping, privatizing, deregulating, trickle-down [policy] that took the greatest economy on the Earth and sent it staggering forward because of their greed and selfishness." Without the EFCA, "the rich will get richer and the rest of us will fend for ourselves."

Perhaps Stern's tirade drowned out the noise of my letter, but the result, as I said, was almost zip, even though I attached pages listing questionable facts regarding union activities. Whether anyone actually read the letter is a question mark because a few weeks after sending it, I learned firsthand about how Washington politicians can look the other way when it is convenient for them to do so.

Accompanying several Midwestern business owners, I flew to Washington for an up-close and personal look at the workings of our taxpayer-paid politicians. One I was interested to speak with was Senator Evan Bayh, Democrat from Indiana. To my amazement, his office actually interceded on SEIU's behalf by contacting a client of ours, a large Indianapolis insurance company, to pressure them into dumping EMS as their cleaning contractor. This tactic did not work, but I wondered why Bayh, whom I had voted for in the last election much to the dismay of Republican friends, would do such a thing. It became apparent later when I met Senator Bayh in Washington with a group of Indiana businessmen about EFCA. When I questioned him on the details and history behind EFCA, it was apparent he had little knowledge. We found this to be the case in meeting after meeting with Congressmen and Senators who depended on young idealistic aids to provide information for their decisions. This is similar to what is occurring with current Stimulus, Environmental and Health bills. From what I witnessed on my trip the members of Congress do not have the time to read the bills and instead rely on the opinions of young aids with very little life experience. This is a very frightening scenario, since it appears the aids, and not the elected politicians, are making the decisions on important national issues.

At this point I would like to digress a bit and cover the role of politics and how difficult it is for politicians to sort through the information. I saw first-hand how overwhelming it is for our political representatives during my visit and in personal conversations with several of them since. Unfortunately, politics plays too big a role in this whole scenario, from the standpoint that it is not what is best for people or the country, it is what is best for politicians and their financial backers. However, in all fairness, the politicians in many cases truly do not have a good grasp for the facts, because they are besieged by so many special interest groups. I empathize with the position of those who are trying to do the right thing and not succumb to these groups.

Unfortunately to special interest groups and unions, employees are no more than pawns in a chess game that is all about money. I know from personal experience as EMS was not allowed to bid on a series of buildings because EMS is non-union. This particular company underwrites a substantial amount of the SEIU health care insurance business and, in turn, has intimate connections with people in Congress who will vote on the Employee Free Choice Act. Obviously, if the SEIU can put enough pressure financially on this company to restrict non-union companies from bidding, it theoretically will also be able to place pressure on the company's congressional connections to vote for the Employee Free Choice Act, without regard to whether the bill is necessary or desired by the American public. In my estimation there is a conflict of interest, which needs to be addressed.

So how does this affect employees? Well if I have not mentioned it before, this is a good time to relate that the SEIU is in favor of Health Care reform as it stands to benefit in several ways. It will benefit of course at the expense of the very people it professes to protect. First, the SEIU is hopeful that the current administration, which benefited tremendously from union support during the recent campaign, will supposedly propose that your company health care benefits be taxed unless you receive such benefits through a union program—in which case they would not be taxable. This would be an immense advantage for union organizers. Does it seem fair to you that unions obtain an unfair advantage at your expense? Probably not, but it is union payback for campaign support.

Second, the SEIU pushes for full-time people in all contracts. Why? Not just so people have more take-home pay, but also because they can sell them health care insurance, charge higher dues, and put more money into union coffers, which in turn is used to elect politicians who push new laws that favor unions and their maniacal need for new membership growth, all at employee expense. Obviously this will provide an uneven playing field, just as EFCA would if passed, and place unwanted pressure on individuals and companies to be unionized whether or not they have an interest!

During my visit to Washington D.C., our contingency chatted with, among others, Senator Richard Lugar (R-Indiana), and Congressmen Mike Pence and Dan Burton, Indiana Republicans. Besides meeting with the politicians, we talked to legislative assistants who appeared to know little about us, why we were there, or the EFCA.

While passing by the office of the Senate Majority Leader Harry Reid's office, one of my colleagues suggested I stop in and pay Senator Harry my respects. Never afraid to take on a challenge unless it involves an opponent giving me few too strokes as a handicap in a golf game, I marched through the door, told a young secretary who I was, and asked to see Senator Reid if he was not too busy shining President Obama's shoes. Just kidding, of course, but as the President is such an advocate of the EFCA along with his Vice President, who knows what good ol' Harry might be doing based on the pressure exerted by Stern and the SEIU, strong contributors to any democratic cause regardless of its merit.

Although I was told Senator Harry was not available, a nice young man (very young), acting as a legislative aide of some sort agreed to speak with me. We sat in a cute little office and I began to give him my reasons for opposing the EFCA. As I spoke, I noticed he had a fondness for a nearby wall while glancing from time to time at his lap. If he had yawned, I wouldn't have been surprised, but instead he simply nodded although I believed he was not hearing a word I said. Finally, I decided enough was enough, and said, "You don't get it, do you?" His face jerked to attention, and he replied, "What do you mean. Hey, we are not your enemy." I quickly said, "I didn't say that, but you don't even know what I am talking about and could care less." Realizing this meeting was going nowhere, I thanked him for talking to me, shook his hand, and left shaking my head in bewilderment at our political process. When I returned to my business colleagues, I told them of the experience. Not one was surprised.

Whether the meetings made a dent in anyone's perception of the EFCA was unknown, but at least we had attempted to make a difference. An ally in our opposition to the pending legislation is the National Right to Work Committee (NRTWC.org), 2.2 million members strong. Their purpose: "dedicated to the principle that all American must have the right to join a union if they choose to, but none should ever be forced to affiliate with a union in order to get or keep a job." Amen, my belief exactly, since any organization that "combats compulsory unionism" is a friend to the worker. And a friend it was when the NRWC spoke up in late March when news hit the ground that Costco, Whole Foods, and Starbucks were agreeing to a "compromise" regarding the check card provisions supported by the SEIU.

One argument proposed by the NRWC, besides the apparent elimination of the secret ballot election, is one which is not considered when the EFCA is debated, which is mandatory arbitration. This is the absolute requirement that if a "first" contract between an employer and employee appears impossible after 90 days, the matter will be decided by compulsory and binding arbitration with no opportunity for appeal in the courts. As the NRWC pointed out,

"Ending secret ballots is just the beginning of the evils of this legislation. Once workers are bullied into union ranks without even a secret ballot, union officials would make outrageous demands and—a mere 90 days later—Obama Administration bureaucrats will be empowered to step in and 'solve the problem,' ultimately imposing the terms and conditions of employment on the workers and the companies." Does this sound fair? Of course not, companies, employees, and unions should all have the benefit of the right to appeal to our system of law. Why should it be any other way?

To show their distaste for these types of opposing views, SEIU's website posted a scathing report on a Small Business Meeting held in Washington D.C. on March 25. Dismissing the event as pure Republican propaganda, they chastised the comment from Senator Orin Hatch (R-Utah): "[Free Choice] sure seems like an Armageddon to me." And they were even tougher on former Labor Solicitor Eugene Scalia. He believed if the act was passed, "union members would surround employees in parking lots." How true this statement was based on EMS's experience during the war with SEIU.

As the debate continues, I'm with those who want the truth to win out. The EFCA legislation appears to have slowed in the Senate providing some hope more investigation will be permitted regarding the merits of the act. But the SEIU is a very powerful, well-financed, and politically connected organization with ties to the highest office in our land, making the fight to stop the EFCA foreboding at best.

While I hold my breath that EFCA will be defeated as more senators learn the truth, SEIU apparently is back in action. Stern wants to win, and will attempt to do so at all cost. Just when I thought we were free of the tentacles of the union, they kicked us in the pants on tax day, 2009 by distributing a flyer outside Market Tower titled "Protecting Freedom is Everybody's Responsibility." Below these words were "But EMS—the Janitorial company that cleans Market Tower—is undermining those freedoms. Region 16 of the

NLRB has found that EMS violated the law of the land by: Illegally refusing to reinstate janitors who were engaged in a protected Unfair Labor Practice (UPL) Strike," and "threatening and interrogating low-wage janitors who speak up for a better life."

Regardless of the authenticity of the claims (including the fact that we have since been absolved of any wrongdoing), and the accompanying protest complete with bullhorns, children, large signs, and flyers, this incident reminded me once again of one clear truth—Stern and the SEIU were not giving up. The war continues as I remind myself each day of his words, "We like conversation, but we embrace confrontation."

Rebuttal of EFCA: A Modern Day True Story

As the EFCA weaves its way through Congress, continued misinformation is released daily by the SEIU and others who oppose companies like EMS. This occurs despite multiple examples existing where the EFCA way of life simply is not workable.

One such example occurred in April 2009 at a steel mill in Ohio. This time the union was not the SEIU, but the Machinists Union. It was attempting to unionize 20 of our workers.

Cause for the unrest, one that came with much surprise as we had never heard a discouraging word from the workers, was tied to the fact that more than two thousand plant workers, because of the tough economic conditions, had been laid off. When the union replaced our workers with twice as many steel workers, the cleaning was not done properly and our workers were asked to return to their jobs. The Machinists Union did not care for this turn of events and decided to attempt to organize our employees. An election was called for where the union promised the moon and pressured the workers into signing union cards. Because EFCA is not law yet, a secret-ballot election was called for, a procedure permitting us to speak to the employees about the EMS position while not degrading the union. If EFCA would have been law we would have been negotiating a contract instead of preparing to meet with our employees concerning the upcoming election!

As required by law, the election would be held within 42 days. According to the act mandates, we chatted with the employees during meetings while the union took them out for chicken wings and beer. I wondered if we should have bought some beer (something not permissible by law on our side) as well but the union had the evening hours all tied up. We were very careful not to promise anything in contrast to the union's ability to do so. And we had to document everything said so as to keep a record; the union did not. During the first meeting, I read a letter prepared by the attorneys, but I hated doing so, because it was so impersonal. The next time I used a prepared outline with more personal words about why I loved EMS and why I thought the employees did not need the union when we were dedicated to protecting their rights all down the line.

When we discovered that many of our employees were being followed all day by an organizer named Roy, we worried that his influence and pressure would win out. This had caused many to sign the union cards along with promises of double the wages, an unrealistic promise if ever there were one. As the employees listened to me it was evident in their eyes they did not realize that just because they signed cards they were not committed to voting for the union during the private secret-ballot election. It was also easy to tell they did not know all of the facts and the consequences of becoming union. Meeting by meeting, it was clear the tide was turning in our favor through interest in what I had to say. Imagine if the EFCA had been in place. The pressure on the employees would have been absolutely incredible with tough steel workers watching the process to see if everyone stood in lock step with union demands. And, most importantly, we would have never had the chance to speak to the employees about our company position. Instead, the wings and beer chats would have been the only information the employees received, certainly only one side of the story.

When election day arrived April 29, 2009, I held my breath as the time neared for the results to be announced. While we were not dealing with Stern and the SEIU, I knew they would be watching closely to see if our employees chose the Machinists Union over me. If we lost, I could expect more harassment, more intimidation, more threats, more flyers, more handbills, more nasty customer letters, more phony NLRB and OSHA charges, and more embarrassing media moments where I was labeled anti-union and anti-American. The war would continue for who knew how long in spite of my attempts to end it in a peaceful and professional manner.

After the secret-ballot election, the vote was two to one against unionization. Because the union would have never petitioned for an election without 70 percent of the employees signing union cards, this meant we turned around the minds of a majority of the workers. And we did it with the truth, through old-fashioned, friendly, informational meetings (no harassment or intimidation as is often claimed) where the workers heard the facts and could ask any questions they wished. What better example of democracy is there, I ask? Bless those workers for their belief in EMS. Their support is an inspiration, one that will keep me fighting the fight against those who intend to stomp on employee rights.

The results are also proof positive that the current NLRA process works if both sides abide by the law and that EFCA is not only unnecessary, but a ploy by the SEIU and others to stop their sliding membership rolls. Hats off to the Machinists Union for conducting the campaign honestly and by the book, unlike the Corporate Campaign process that the SEIU uses to browbeat employees and companies into unwanted unionism.

Even better, the machinist representatives were gentle-men when they lost, just as I would have been if I had lost. But they shook hands and left peaceably, even though they had to be disappointed. Democracy in action, I would call it. True democracy.

Acknowledgments

A BOOK IS A COLLECTIVE EFFORT ON THE PART OF MANY PEOPLE AND I thank all of those who have been so important in supporting me through this vicious campaign imposed upon EMS by the SEIU.

First of all, to my wife Barb and my children—thank you—who had to put up with long hours and diversions from family time. As events occurred beyond my control, my mood swings affected us all as I focused on trying to save EMS from oblivion.

To those customers, many of whom had to experience humiliation, defamation, bad public relations, and unwanted exposure, I thank you for standing by my side because I believe you knew it was the proper thing to do.

To our loyal management staff, both the people that report directly to me, and all of the others who work for us nationwide, I value all of you and your contribution to EMS's success and longevity. I know fighting the SEIU has taken my eye off the ball at times and I haven't provided the support I would under normal circumstances. Thank you for taking up the slack and taking care of our valued customers.

To our nearly five thousand employees in 33 states who work on the front lines every day representing EMS,

I thank you with the reminder that you are meaningful and that without you the world would be a pretty messy place in which to live. I salute you and your dedication to quality every single day.

To our company attorneys—thank you for putting in countless hours and standing by us with solid legal advice as we paraded through the landmines SEIU set for us. I would have been lost without you.

To Mark Shaw, a great author in his own right whose ingenious creativity and guidance made this story come to life.

To Bob Radigan, Sanibel, Florida, realtor for all the time and effort in creating an outstanding cover design.

To the media who have heard my story and publicized it, I thank you as I do those politicians who have stood up, checked out the facts thoroughly, and then taken a stand against tyranny, threat, intimidation, and pressure from the unions who embrace organizing tactics that are intimidating and Un-American. You know the difference between right and wrong and your integrity has shown through during this difficult time.